A MALVERN TREASURY

220 illustrations, 46 in colour

Cover photograph - sculpture of Anne Savage, c1590, Malvern Priory

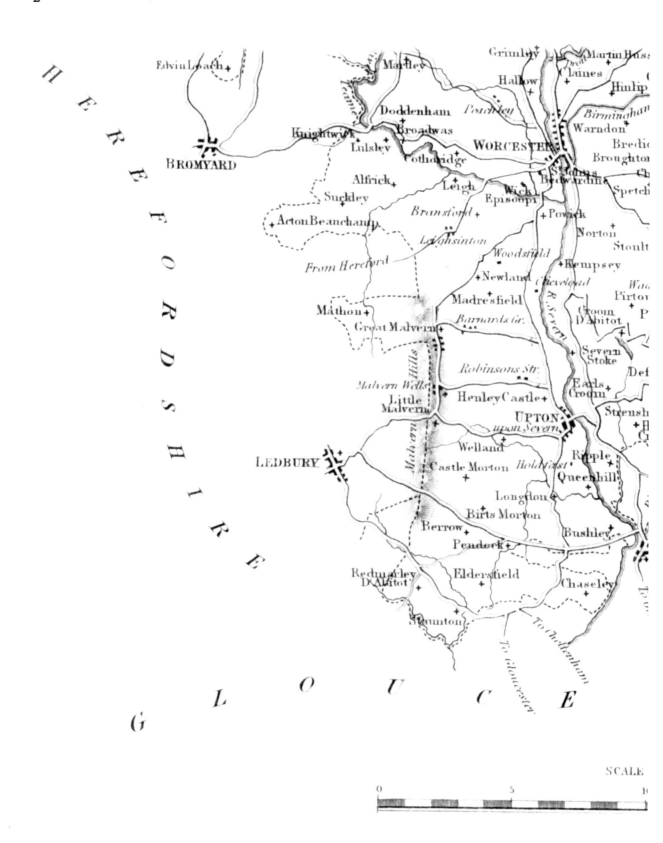

Southern section of the map of Worcestershire

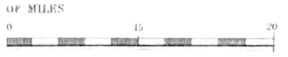

Lewis's Topographical Dictionary 1831

A MALVERN TREASURY

an Illustrated History
of its People and Places,
Troubles and Treasures,
in Fact and Fable

by Rose Garrard

Garrard Art Publications; Malvern; England

Garrard Art Publications

A MALVERN TREASURY

© Rose Garrard 2010
Second Edition

All Rights Reserved

Photographs as credited

ISBN: 978-1-905795-56-7

Design Layout by Rose Garrard

Digital Production by Aspect Design
Printed by Aspect Design
89 Newtown Road, Malvern, Worcs. WR14 1AN
United Kingdom
Tel:01684 561567
Email: books@aspect-design.net

Garrard Art Publications; Malvern; England

ACKNOWLEDGEMENTS

My sincerest thanks for all the support given on this self-published venture by those who have generously contributed help, information, and images, including Brian Iles, Jonathan Penley, Peter Smith, Paul Farrer, Mike Austin, Christine and Roland Bannister, David and Dinah Prentice, Worcester City Museums, the British Museum, the Imperial War Museum, the Malvern Museum, Malvern Library, Malvern Priory and Malvern Gazette, Sue Smith and all at Aspect Design. I also gratefully acknowledge the many written texts listed in the bibliography on page 176 that have made this book possible. Some of the illustrations included here are out of copyright or are in the public domain, and others appear by kind permission of their owners, or are permitted under the Wikipedia Creative Commons Licence. Every attempt has been made to trace and obtain permission to reproduce all images and credit them. The author will be happy to correct any omissions in future printings.

Garrard Art Publications

A MALVERN TREASURY

an Illustrated History of its People and Places, Troubles and Treasures, in Fact and Fable

LIST OF CONTENTS

Window in Priory House, 1888, now Malvern Hills District Council House

INTRODUCTION

Why *"A Malvern Treasury"*? There have been many books on aspects of Malvern's past, but only a few have attempted to record its full ancient to modern history, from the creation of the hills to the present day. The last of these histories was published almost twenty years ago. As none of these few are now in print, in 2008 I was asked if I would consider writing a new history book. At first, not being a historian, I was reluctant to undertake this daunting task, but as the evenings grew darker my curiosity led me to begin re-reading the oldest 19th century books in my collection, sketching an outline on the computer and then researching further. Although the previous histories had created valuable academic records, the density of their detail often made them difficult reading. Also, these earlier authors did not have the advantages of digital technology and so had included few images in their books and none in colour. I was hooked. As well as the important events and local legends, I wanted the book to be an intriguing historical record of some of the many treasures to be found here, the rare images, the precious objects, people and places in the district. Two years later, I hope that this illustrated book will provide a pleasurable introduction to the fascinating story of Malvern, its joys and troubles in both fact and fable.

Rose Garrard 2010.

Carved owl, 1888, in the Council House

Sea of clouds below the Malvern Hills *courtesy John Bibby*

Chapter I

Finding Fossils and Fortunes

he very hard binary granites of the Malvern Hills were forced to the earth's surface as molten rock almost seven hundred million years ago, by tectonic pressure, earthquakes and violent volcanic eruptions. The hot magma that had formed deep within the earth's crust was pushed upwards, cooling slowly on the surface to create some of the oldest and hardest rocks on earth, later surrounded by the Silurian Sea.

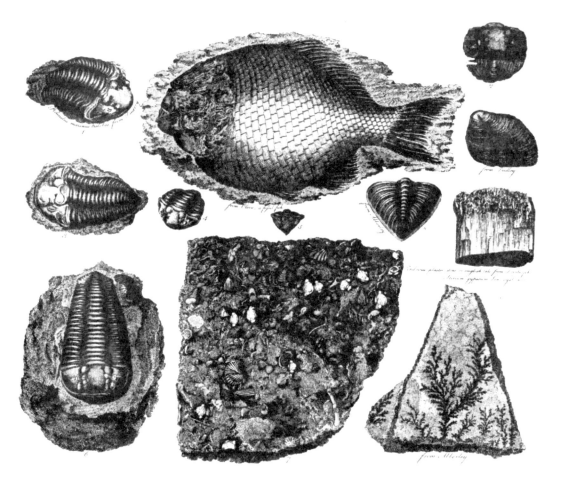

Fossilised sea creatures found in the county, from Nash's Worcestershire, 1799

After many millions of years, this nine mile long hill ridge firstly became a track-way for prehistoric hunters, later the boundary between warring

14

tribes, then between feuding landowners, and it now divides the peaceful counties of Herefordshire and Worcestershire. The most recent tremor felt along this Dudley fault-line was early in the morning of 23rd September 2002, when some residents in the Malverns were woken by a low, deep rumbling and ran into the streets as their houses shook.

There are magical mornings on the Malvern Hills, when you find you are walking above a sheet of clouds that stretches around every protruding hilltop as far as the horizon. Very occasionally, in strong sunlight, your giant shadow may be thrown far across this white surface, a phenomenon known as a *"brochan spectre"*. The sunshine diffracts around your body creating a halo of colours and projects your enlarged shadow inside the circle of surrounding light, onto the cloud below; an amazing sight.

This flat sea of clouds brings echoes of the ancient Silurian Sea, which lapped the shores of this granite ridge six hundred million years ago, shaping the landscape of the Malverns. At that time the hills and ridges below were islands and coral reefs in this warm, shallow, tropical sea. In 2007, whilst Raglan House in West Malvern was being rebuilt on Westminster Bank, the instability of the Victorian building was explained when the remains of a shingle beach and small marine fossils were discovered beneath the old foundations. From here you can walk down Croft Bank into Herefordshire and along the wooded ridge below, formed by the fossilised remains of a coral reef. At Fossil Bank below Wyche Cutting or down an ancient track nearby, called the Purlieu, tiny fossilised sea creatures can still be found and these were quarried during the 18th century to extract their lime in the nearby kilns. *"The western declivities of the hills contain a bed of limestone, which contains an almost infinite variety of marine productions, particularly the remains of shell-fish; such as cockles and muscles of various sizes and fish encrusted with stony concretion. These, together with corals, cornua Ammionis, sponges, vertebrae of large fish, &c., leave no doubt that these hills, or part of them, were once under water."* (Mary Southall, A Description of Malvern, 1825)

As the Silurian sea receded, leaving the hills and Severn valley exposed, the surrounding landscape was left with treacherous marshes, which gradually seeded with trees to become dense wet forests. The sea returned twice more to completely cover the hills. The forest trees decayed in the swamps, to eventually form the coal deposits of Dudley. The area then became a vast saline lake, which evaporated leaving huge salt deposits at Droitwich, while the remaining sand and mud formed the familiar red sandstones and clays of the county. Lastly came the Ice Age, with moving glaciers that carried large boulders from Scotland down the channel between the Malverns and the Cotswolds. After the great thaw the seas retreated to reveal the present course of the river Severn flowing

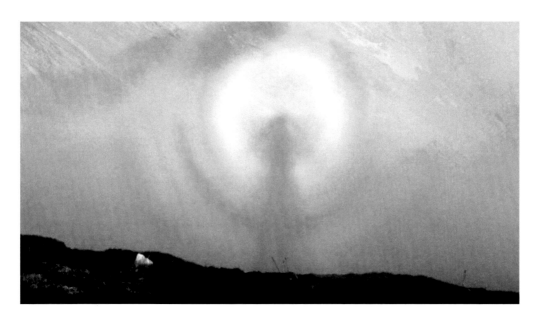

'Brochan Spectre' on mist below the top of Lakeland Fells courtesy Quentin Harding

Fossilised limestone strata from the Silurian Sea, in a quarry at West Malvern

through a marshy plain, which soon became thickly wooded and gradually filled with wild animals. Fault lines separate the Pre-Cambrian Malvern Hills' ridge from a variety of younger sedimentary layers in the valleys along both sides, formed by this ancient sea bed.

Rain falling on the surface of the Malvern Hills soaked into their thin soil, percolating through the numerous tiny cracks in the crowns into the fissures and hollows in the insoluble granite beneath, creating aquifers of stored water within and beneath the ridge. The weight of the percolating rain pressing down on the deeper water inside the porous granite, pushed it back up along the fault line, against the sedimentary layers, forming numerous pure springs. Today the water emerges at over 100 points as fault springs, creating a necklace of water sources around the entire hill range. Most of these springs absorb minute amounts of minerals from the sedimentary layers, the Silurian rocks on the west or the Keuper rocks on the east side. These minerals give various slight flavours to each fault-spring. But at least two famous sources, Holy Well, and St Ann's Well, are exceptions, as they actually arise above the fault line, directly from the insoluble Pre-Cambrian granite and so are the most renowned for their purity, lack of minerals and clean taste.

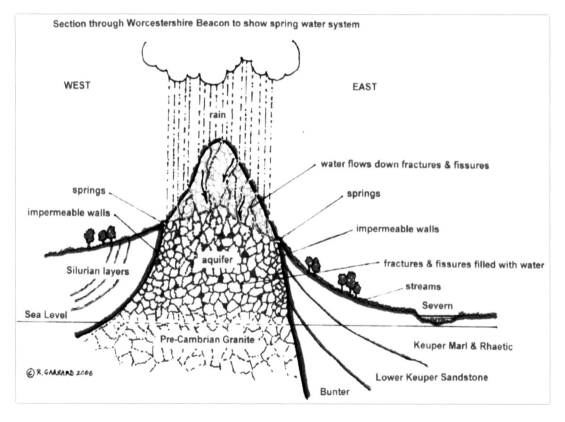

In the 19th century it was suggested that the name Malvern is pure Gaelic – Mial-chiurn – pronounced Mal-vurne, being literally "hill of fountains". Certainly the hills once sparkled with the streams from all these springs, which flowed down towards the river Severn in the east or into the lush western valleys. But in the last one hundred and fifty years most have been 'harvested' to collect their prolific waters, by piping them underground. However, today you can still drink from twelve public spouts, pure spring water sources around the Malvern Hills.

Over 15,000 years ago the river Severn brought the very first few

Palaeolithic explorers or Old Stone Age people here, who probably travelled upstream by using small coracles, boats which could easily be carried, along with their weapons and tools of unpolished knapped flint. *"Severn fishermen on the higher reaches of the river still construct their shell-like boats of wicker framework, covered with oiled cloth or leather, on the ancient British plan." (Historic Worcestershire, by W Salt Brassington, 1894)*

Palaeolithic flint tool, actual size, possibly for stripping bark from arrow shafts. Found by the author among dredgings from the river near Upton on Severn in 1950

By Neolithic times, 2,000 years before Christ's birth, the river had become the major travel and trade route through this dangerous wilderness. Arising above the dense forests and marshes, the bare hill summits then began to attract early visitors, now carrying finely finished and polished flint tools, who used the ridge as a safer overland travel route linked to other ridge ways. Today the popularly held view is that Malvern means 'bare hills', due to the limited plant and tree growth on the thin soil over most of the granite peaks. *"The name is probably derived from the British word 'Moel' signifying bald, and 'Wern', Alders, imputing a bald hill with alders at the bottom, or rather from 'Moel', which in British signifies a mountain." (Dr T. Nash, History of Worcestershire, 1799)* A Neolithic flint axe found near St James' Church in West Malvern was on one ancient land route, which once passed along Croft Ridge at Cother Wood, through today's Croft Farm, up to the Malvern Hill ridge above, then south to the Hereford Beacon and beyond. It tracked along several other ridge ways running from the Abberley Hills to the Forest of

Dean. There was also an early overland route to the north of Malvern, avoiding the wooded swamps, where early traders carried flint goods between the regions of North Wales and Wessex.

A series of ancient burial sites have been found along the northerly hills. On the summit of the North Hill itself, a collapsed burial mound or tumulus was described in 1856, but has long since disappeared from view. *"There appears an immense grave, part of which is entire. The narrow part appears to have fallen in. The old inhabitants of Malvern call it the Giant's Grave. It has a very peculiar appearance; by the side is the form of a cross."* (Notes and Queries for Worcestershire, John Noake, 1856) On the saddle between North Hill and End Hill, a flint arrow-head was discovered in the 19th century. A table-like mound was also recorded on Table Hill, and mid-way along the ridge, on the top of Pinnacle Hill, the circular hollows from two Bronze Age burial mounds are still just discernable, above the source of Holy Well.

On the Worcestershire Beacon, as well as a flint axe and scrapers, some human bones and a nearby cremation burial were excavated in November 1849 and the remains given to the British Museum, but apparently these have since been lost. The two burials were found when a mapping survey was being undertaken by the Royal Ordnance Corps and a Private Harkin was excavating to find the trigonometric marker stone from a previous survey. On the very top of the hill he first discovered part of a human skull and then nearby, the 'beaker' burial of a cremated adult. This was covered by an upturned pottery 'pygmy' cup or urn dating from between 1600 to 760 BC, *"On uncovering the rock, about nine inches below the surface, just on the outer edge, the small urn was found in a cavity of the rock, with some bones and ashes. The urn*

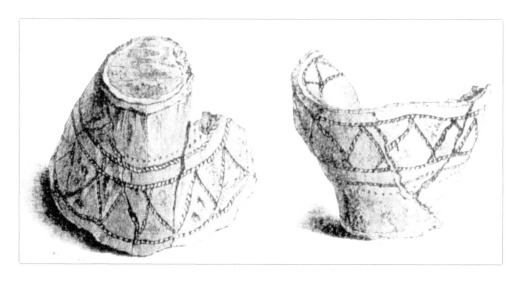

'Pygmy' cup covering a cremation, found on the Worcestershire Beacon in 1849

was placed in an inverted position, covering part of the ashes. ... The conspicuous position of the site where this deposit was found, being the highest point of the hill range in the part adjoining Great Malvern, seems to indicate that it was the resting place of some chieftain or person of note at an early period in our history." (Antiquities & Folklore of Worcestershire by Jabez Allies 1852)

In 1910, in Herefordshire, just below this northerly group of hills, a further fifteen Bronze Age cremation burials, a bronze axe-head and pottery urns dating from 1000 BC, were excavated at Southend Farm near Cradley Brook, Mathon. It was believed that twice as many more burials still lay undiscovered in the vicinity. Beneath these finds, other interments from the Early Bronze Age were uncovered, along with flints and part of a quern for grinding grain, proving that the site had been in use for many hundreds of years, well into the Iron Age. In 1937 a mid Bronze Age pottery urn was found here, patterned with incised parallel lines, chevrons, and dots. Some claimed that the meaning of the name Mathon was *"place of treasure"*, suggesting that previous generations had discovered ancient valuables here. *"A notion has long prevailed that much treasure has been lost or deposited in the Malvern Hills; but from whence such an opinion originated we are at a loss to conjecture. However, a quantity of silver coin was found, about 40 years back, on the western side of the hills, in the parish of Mathon. It is said it amounted to a considerable value; but there are no further particulars of it."* (John Chambers, A General History of Malvern, 1817)

On the other side of the northerly hills another Bronze Age axe-head was excavated in 1780 in Malvern Link, from many feet underground. It was also dated to 1000 BC and was of a very similar design to the Mathon axe, a type known as a 'socketed pulsave', with cast sockets and a loop for attachment to a handle with a leather thong. Sadly both weapons have since been lost, although the Malvern Museum has a cast of the Link axe.

Bronze Age axe-head or 'celt' excavated in Malvern Link in 1780

Further south, in 1875 Mr H. Lines, from the Birmingham Archaeological Association, recorded numerous hut circles on Midsummer Hill and on the adjoining Holly Bush Hill, dating from before 450 BC, the earliest known settlement on the Malverns, although many of these remains are no longer visible. 'Duck-stamped' pottery was found here and on Bredon Hill in the Severn Vale and was probably produced locally. Flint axes and scrapers have also been excavated on these prehistoric sites.

Black Samian Ware with swans, distinctive 'duck-stamped' pottery from the Severn Vale, c1000 BC, Courtesy of Steve Burgess 2009

Eventually the original occupants constructed one double rampart surrounding both settlements, for their own protection. The two hills were probably fortified as a place to take shelter in times of crisis, rather than as a permanently occupied site. The ramparts enclose a total of thirty acres of land, including a valley and two springs to ensure a water supply. *"The overflow of two springs, one within and one beyond the protection of the Camp, were conveyed into four small receptacles or tanks to be stored in case of necessity."* (James Mc Kay, British Camp, 1875)

In Victorian times this large camp, enclosing the Holly Bush Ravine, was known as *"Dyn Mawr"*, meaning *"great city"*, and the site was described in detail by James McKay. *"The flank of Midsummer Hill facing the glen, displays eleven concentric oval terraces, one above the other and as many as 214 hut hollows are plainly discernible along these lines, and another 30 may be found by the exercise of a little diligence and patience"* and on Holly Bush Hill he recorded, *"excavations, circular in form, and forty in number, showing the sites of huts once tenanted by Celtic denizens."* (James Mc Kay, The British Camp, 1875)

The dead were interred here too, with three burial mounds and a 'pillow' mound discovered on Holly Bush Hill in 1924, as well as pottery fragments dating from the Early Bronze Age before 450 BC, made by the Dobunni from the La Tene culture of Ancient Britons. The pillow mound was later re-classified as a possible medieval rabbit warren, built to breed *"coneys"* for the table. Rabbits were only introduced into Britain by the Normans after their victory in 1066.

Greek pottery remains have been found in the river Severn, fragments of terracotta amphorae dating from between 700 and 450 BC. Also two pieces from a 'parsnip-shaped' amphora, six millimetres thick, were recently uncovered in an excavation at Picken's End, Hanley Swan. These amphorae were used to import Mediterranean wine and are evidence of the Celtic love of alcohol and perhaps their early trade in slaves. Plato wrote that after crossing the sea, many Greek merchants *"transport the wine by boat up navigable rivers and receive in return for it an incredibly high price; for one jar of wine they receive a slave – a servant in exchange for a drink."*
(The Celts by John Davies, 2000)

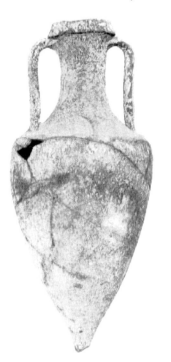

A typical Greek wine amphora, early first century BC

Although it seems there was no Roman settlement on the hills, there is some evidence that the Romans travelled through the hill passes of the Malverns from Droitwich, their most important local settlement when Worcester was only a small village, specialising in iron smelting. Two urns of Roman coins were discovered at Wynds Point and some isolated examples have been found on the upper hill slopes. In 1847 W. S. W. Vaux also recorded *"an important find of Roman coins, unexpectedly made in the parish of Little Malvern by Commissioner Mayne and his sons who were out walking in search of geological items of interest"*. At Bank Farm, West Malvern, Stephen Ballard recalled that before 1918, when Tupsley Field was being ploughed up to plant soft fruits, *"One of the workmen picked up a genuine Roman gold coin here"*.

There have also been small Roman pottery finds in North Malvern. In 1976 remains of kilns, bowls, tankards and flagons dating from 150 AD were excavated from farmland west of Lower Howsell Road. Several Romano-British kilns and many pottery fragments have been discovered in the lower Malvern Link to Newland areas and numerous water-filled clay pits, now lined with trees. Recently archaeologists have also identified an early clay pit near Picken's End in Hanley Swan. This whole area was a major site for the ancient pottery industry that produced Severn Valley Ware in the region until about 300 AD. A little further away, as well as early pottery found recently at Great Buckman Farm, *"pottery and a kiln have been excavated from a villa site at Sandlin Farm, Leigh Sinton"*. *(Brian Smith, A History of Malvern, 1964)*

In 1856 a Late Bronze Age hoard of two hundred and fifty metal ingots, made from Forest of Dean iron ore, was found near the Wyche Pass. This find was uncovered on the hillside beside an ancient route for pack animals that crossed the hills at the Wyche, carrying salt from the Droitwich brine springs to South Wales. These long thin bars were probably intended for use in trading for salt and several of them are on loan to the Malvern Museum. This ancient trade route became part of the Roman *"Upper Saltway"* and the word wyche may derive from the Saxon word *"wich"* for a street or track often associated with salt. *"The inhabitants of this county, and a large adjacent tract of county, were denominated by the Saxons as 'Wiccii'. This title is supposed, and not without plausibility, to have originated in the name of 'Wiches' or 'Wics', the briny springs in which this county is well known to have abounded from the earliest times. The 'Wiches' are said to derive their name from the Saxon word which signifies 'holy'."* (A Concise History and Description of the City and Cathedral of Worcester, by T. Eaton, 1829)

Late Bronze Age rusty iron ingots found on the Malvern Hills

It's thought that the territory of the Wiccia, also spelt Hwicca or Hwicce, coincided with the later Diocese of Worcester, which was founded in about 679. Their lands probably included most of Worcestershire, Gloucestershire and southwest Warwickshire and they became Christians

under the early British Church. Bede tells us that the South Saxon Queen Eafe had been baptised in her own country, the kingdom of the Hwicce. *"Hwicce"* is Old English for a container or cauldron, interpreted to mean *"sacred vessel"*, linked to the shape of the Severn Vale and to the Romano-British regional cult of a goddess holding a water vessel. The name not only survives at Wyche Cutting but also in Droitwich, Wichenford and Wychbury Hill, all in Worcestershire, Wychwood in Oxfordshire, Whichford in Warwickshire, and the newly named Wychavon district.

Recent archaeological finds in Worcestershire

Bronze Age spear head, Bromsgrove, *Courtesy of Portable Antiquities Scheme, British Museum*

La Tene brooch c50 AD, Earls Croome, 3cm
Courtesy of Portable Antiquities Scheme

**Cremation Casket mount c200 AD, 4cm,
Claines** *Courtesy of Portable Antiquities Scheme*

Early Bronze Age axe, Malvern Hills, 12cm
Courtesy of Portable Antiquities Scheme

**Romano-British votive brooch, c50 AD,
Inkberrow, 3cm.** *Portable Antiquities Scheme*

**Anglo-Saxon cruciform and disc
brooches, c700 AD, found in a
gravel pit at Upton Snodsbury**
Courtesy Worcester City Museums

In the 13th century one of the Droitwich salt springs dried up but was believed to have been made to flow again by St Richard of Wyche. He was a Worcestershire man who, against the wishes of Henry III, had become Bishop of Chichester. The King confiscated the revenues of the 'see' and the Bishop became a homeless wanderer, performing his duties whilst also planting, pruning, and grafting fruit trees across his diocese.

For nine years after his death many miracles were reported at his tomb and he was then canonised. St Richard later became the patron saint of the Droitwich salt trade. *"On the day of St Richard, they kept holy-day, and dressed the wells with green boughs and flowers. One year in Presbyterian time, it was discontinued in the civil wars, and after that the spring shrank up, or dried up for some time; so afterwards they revived their annual custom, notwithstanding the power of the Parliament and soldiers, and the salt water returned again, and still continues."* (Lansdown Manuscript, by Aubrey, from Historic Worcestershire, W. Salt Brassington 1894)

Seal of Bishop Richard of Wyche, c1245

The years of work on cutting through the granite hill at the Wyche, to widen and lower this pass into the present roadway, was not begun until 1836 and after this it gradually became known as the Wyche Cutting.

The early Wyche Pass with gas lamp, seen from the Herefordshire side, c1860

Salt works at Droitwich, c1880

19th century women workers making salt blocks at Droitwich

Timber being carted through the Wyche Pass beside High Land Cottage, c1870

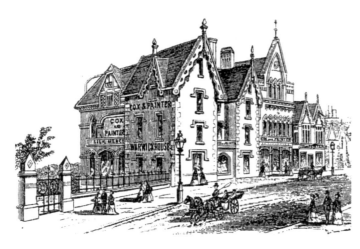

The stone quarried from the cutting was then used to build the long supporting wall, still opposite Warwick House, beside the southern roadway into Great Malvern.

The new Warwick House building with Cox & Painter's store, c1850

The new upper road and steep old Lower Wyche Road up to the Wyche Pass, c1870

There was an ancient spring at the pass, the Primes Spring, which would have been invaluable to the earliest travellers after their steep uphill climb. But when the road was being constructed, the waters were diverted from the grassy bank in front of High Land Cottage to Wyche Spout, a new Victorian water spout, which can still be found on the opposite bank but is now dry, the pipe having been cut off in 1990. In 1930 this water was described as originating from a pure spring flowing directly out of the Archaean granite, like Holy Well and St Ann's Well. At first the new water spout was primarily for the use of the quarrymen, working for the Pyx Granite Company, who lived in the first houses built here in the 1840s, during the construction of the new cutting and tarmacadam roadway. The spring water attracted other villagers to live nearby, who relied on it as their sole source of drinking and domestic water until the 1890s, but the spout still remained a popular water source for a further one hundred years. It is now known to have been Well

Dressed occasionally until July 1978, the last time by the local newsagent, Mrs Amhurst, who created a large panel of flower petals in the style of her Derbyshire origins, to celebrate the pure water.

On the Malvern Hills a long tradition of Well Dressing has existed since at least the 12th century and today about thirty spring water sites are beautifully well-dressed annually by local residents. This tradition was revived by Cora Weaver in the autumn of 1993 and has been organised by Malvern Spa Association since 1998, now held on May Day.

Well Dressing on Wyche Spout 'tump' in 1978 courtesy of D Beard

Well Dressing of the Wyche Spout, organised by Malvern Spa Association, 2006

The Colwall Stone, still at the crossroads, is associated with legends of giants

Chapter II

Druidic Legends and Roman Legions

sing known social models, the Romans categorised the varied Druidic peoples of Britain into named clans or tribes, each often with a single 'capital city' and a 'king'. In the second century after Christ, it was Ptolemy who first named the Iron Age Druidic people living in and around the Cotswolds as the Dobunni, although they were not a single tribe united under one leader. The Dobunni were a diverse and peaceable people, not a warlike group, mainly made up of farmers and craftspeople, living in small independent villages and making simple pottery and metal objects. The boundaries of their territories varied and at some periods stretched into parts of today's Worcestershire and Herefordshire from North Somerset, Gloucestershire and Warwickshire. Their largest population was concentrated at the site of present day Cirencester, with most of their impressive fortified camps or defensive hill-forts built to the south of the Severn Estuary, stretching north east from Bristol.

After creating their enclosure on Hollybush and Midsummer Hills, in about 250 to 100 BC they constructed the fortified hilltop of *"British Camp"* on the Herefordshire Beacon, as a sanctuary to protect them from the attacks of other warring clans. But these Druidic people normally lived in the fertile Severn vale below, near *"wet places"*, which were often also used for their religious and ritual purposes, and they are said to have regarded some of the prolific water sources on the Malvern Hills as sacred. They revered the waters of rivers, marshes, springs and pools, often breaking precious sharp objects, including spears, swords and brooches, as sacrificial offerings placed in the water. *"Several old finds*

Bronze Age Celtic sword c300 BC, dredged from the river Severn, 40cm
Courtesy Worcester City Museums, 2010

from the river Severn itself are of great interest because of their antiquity and because they suggest that the river had a role in the prehistoric period as a place for votive offerings. Bronze Age weapons have been dredged from the river just below Diglis in Worcester."(Severn Bankside Survey, Worcestershire Archaeological Service 2008)

As ancient springs were meeting places where the Celtic population gathered daily to collect water and perform Druidic rites, the first Christian missionaries began preaching at these sites. When they arrived in the Malverns from Ireland and Europe, they used the springs to baptise the local pagan population and so the waters became known as 'holy', including the Holy Well in Malvern Wells and Holywell near Storridge. The latter was formerly known as *"Hwitan Wyllan"* or the White Well, perhaps with connections to the early Cistercian missionaries, 'white friars' who wore white habits. *"In the course of time when the Christian Missionary came upon the scene, he preached and taught at places where men had gathered – that is, round these springs of water. Then the converts would need baptism, and so the well was made use of for that purpose, and probably its old heathen dedication was changed into a Christian one from that day onwards. As the ages went on, the memory of the holy man who had taught Christianity on any given spot was treasured up, and the well where he had given the sacrament of baptism was looked upon as something sacred. When sickness came these waters were used with faith and were said to have a healing virtue."* (Dom Ethelbert Horne c.1915)

Ditchford Spring or Mary's Well in Little Malvern and a number of other Malvern sources were also considered as holy wells. These included Moorall's Well, now lost, and Walm's Well below British Camp, both of which were said to have been named after the earliest missionaries here from Europe. In 1875 James McKay wrote, *"In Colwall we have Walm's Well, which yet is much resorted to by the rustics, on account of, what they regard as its admirable curative properties; and Moorall's Well, which though less known now, was formerly quite as celebrated. These are unquestionably Ancient British names, and there can be small doubt that they are so called from the first Silurian Christian Missionaries, who took up their posts in the mountain passes of the Malvern Hills. ... The Silurian Missionaries Moorall and Walm stood by what we now call Burstner's Cross and Rye Cross, endeavouring to allure the Celts from the rites and superstitions of their Druid faith."*

Walm's Well, Wa'am's Well or St Waum's Well is in News Wood, below Clutters Cave on the south-western slopes of British Camp.

Although now hidden beneath a concrete container, this is one of the most ancient surviving well sites in the Malverns, traced back to between 250 and 100 BC. At about that time the Dobunni people built a broad track-way to their newly fortified hilltop of British Camp, passing beside this well, which was essential for their survival as there were no springs within the hill defences. There were other accessible water sources further away on the slopes, including several springs on the eastern slopes, since engulfed by the Victorian reservoir completed in 1895, plus Pewtress Spring in Upper Colwall, now enclosed and bottled by Coca-Cola and renamed Primeswell. *"Surely we may picture woad-dyed Britons trooping from the British Camp to see little children baptised in the Gullet stream, or in the sparkling wells on the slope of the hill, or hastening to the banks of Sabrina* (River Severn) *to listen to the discussions between the fathers of the British Church, which had been established by the self-denying labours of Moorall and Walm, the Silurian missionaries to Dyn Mawr, the great city of the Holly Bush Ravine."* (James Mc Kay, The British Camp, 1875)

In 1630 at the important hill pass beside British Camp, known first as Wyndiate, Wynd Gate or later Wynds Point, Thomas Tayler was digging a boundary ditch around his cottage near Burstner's Cross, when he made a rare and valuable discovery. He uncovered *"a beautiful gold coronet*

Burstner's Cross, hotel and quarry at Wynds Point, British Camp, c1850, Bannisters

or armlet, deep set with precious gems" and sold it to Mr Hill, a goldsmith in Gloucester for £37, apparently a large reward. But the goldsmith then sold it on to a London jeweller in Lombard Street for

£250, who removed the stones and sold them for £1,500, a large fortune. Various suggestions have been made for the origin of this treasure, including, *"That this was the diadem of an Ancient British prince, who might have been slain in some contest near the spot"*, or that it may have been buried *"by the British King Margadud in his flight from the Saxon leader Athelstan in pre-Roman times"*, but as the jeweller broke it up to sell on the stones, we shall never know.

Burstner's Cross was probably once the site of an ancient preaching cross and nearby was a major spring water site, a holy well and pool named Moorall's Well. The waters of this pool *"close to the Cross Inn"*, now the Malvern Hills Hotel, were believed to have healing powers and even in Victorian times the site was described as being *"like the pool of Bethesda"*, thronged with sick people bathing and lying around its edges. Beside the same crossroads in 1847, when searching for fossils near Wynds Point quarry, a fifteen year old girl and a Mr Fletcher uncovered two pottery urns containing two hundred and fifty coins, *"a large find of Roman coins dating between AD 286 and 311, some of them apparently in mint-state."* *(Worcestershire in English History, Alec Macdonald 1943)* They had been minted in Treves, London, Aquileia, and Carthage. These coins were bought by Mr Cox-Magnus, an antiquarian, and entrusted to the British Museum, but efforts in 1914 to have them returned to the Malvern Museum were unsuccessful as apparently they had since been lost.

The British Camp swimming pool in the 1920's, below the hotel and café hut

The actual site of this holy well is also unknown today, but possibly Moorall's Well was in the south-western woods below the Malvern Hills Hotel. In the early 20th century there was an elegant public swimming pool here with a lions head water spout fed from a prolific spring, but this source has since been piped underground and the pool demolished. It's not known why these treasures were buried here, whether they might have been hidden as offerings of thanks to the nearby healing spring, or even if the coins might be evidence that the Romans once used this pass.

The fortifications of the British Camp itself form an impressive stepped silhouette on the hill ridge above. Here thousands of tons of soil and

rock on the Herefordshire Beacon have been moved by the Dobunni

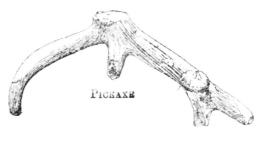

using primitive hand tools, to create a formidable ziggurat of huge ditches and ramparts, originally topped by wooden palisades.   The outer rampart encloses forty-four acres of land, is a mile and a quarter long and, despite erosion still, measures thirty feet from the base of its inner ditch to the top of the next rampart. Although the flat summit had long been

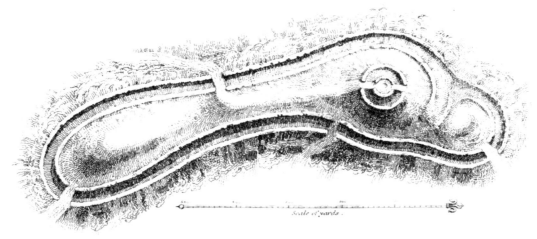

believed to have supported a circular prehistoric wooden 'citadel', in the early 20th century Sir Mortimer Wheeler and other eminent scholars claimed that it had been the site of a later Norman keep and that the overall shape of the camp, with its two wings, is typical of a Norman castle with two baileys. However, no archaeological evidence to support this theory has yet been found and the only excavated pottery fragments have been dated to before 100 BC and to the 16th century.

The Red Earl's Dyke, a boundary ditch running along the ridge of the hills, was thought to have been built in about 1287 by Gilbert de Clare, the 'Red Earl' of Gloucester, to prevent deer escaping back over the summit during a boundary dispute with the Bishop of Hereford. But now archaeologists believe *"the Shire Ditch, or at least part of it, must be prehistoric - possibly dating to the late Bronze Age (about 1000 BC). The 'Red Earl', it seems, just refurbished an existing boundary earthwork, rather than starting from scratch".* (English Heritage Newsletter, 2009)

The Victorians were fascinated by the name Malvern and suggested that its original meaning was *"the seat of judgement"*. Since then, some local people have continued to believe that the flat summit of the camp was created by the Celts to house a Druidic high court. *"The author of a history of Brecknockshire (Jones) incidentally mentions that Malvern is but another form of the Welsh words Moel-y-varn, which means "a high court" or "judgement seat" and this is the etymology, which, on mature deliberation, all persons regarding the early circumstances of the district*

will accept. "The principal and earliest use to which the summit of this hill was appropriated was the assemblage of the Druids, when they acted in their three-fold capacities as legislators, priests and judges; a high court of council and judgement". If this be really the meaning of the word Malvern, what more reasonable than to conclude that the Herefordshire Beacon, which, in former times was the most important point of the range, contained within the protection of its fortress, a seat of judgement." (James Mc Kay, The British Camp, 1875)

An ancient relief of Druids from a burial mound in Autun, France, engraving 1845

In Roman accounts, Druid priests are variously described from brutal and barbaric, to *"wise judges, philosophers and peacemakers"* and according to Julius Caesar, after he came to Britain in 55 and 54 BC, were respected for their study of *"the stars and their motion, the extent of the world and of our earth and the nature of things"*. Although there is no direct evidence for the Druidic use of British Camp, today there is also a widespread local belief that the nearby valley of the Whiteleaved Oak was a most important sacred woodland site, central to the priestly rituals of all the Druidic tribes of Britain. *"Within the memory of living men an oak existed in the little valley, round which superstitions still lingered, which were unquestionably of Druidic origin. Its leaves were dotted over with blotches of white, and their size, arrangement and number were taken as omens by the credulous rustic, of the fortunes, good or bad, which the fates had in store for him. The peasantry residing hard by could give no reason for the dread mysterious tremor which seized them when penetrating at dusk or nightfall its uncanny recesses; nor does it always strike the stranger, of a better class, that all these weird superstitions owed their true origins to the traditional associates of the place, with the rites and ceremonies once celebrated in the sheltered bosom of the glen by the Druid priests."* (James Mc Kay, British Camp, 1875)

The centre of the hamlet of Whiteleaved Oak is the meeting point of the three counties, Gloucestershire, Herefordshire and Worcestershire, which Alfred Watkins claimed to also be the conjunction of numerous ley lines.

The earliest written record of a great tree called *"the white leved Oake"* seems to have been made by Henry Dingly in 1584, when he was beating the boundary of the Chase. This white-leaved oak attracted so many visitors that it was felled by David Ricardo in the 18th century to discourage sightseers. Many normal oaks still grow in the vicinity, and a small stream flows down this beautiful narrow valley at the southernmost end of the range, between the Ragged-stone and Chase End, beyond the fortified hills. There are now said to be three white-leaved oaks here; one was planted beside a tiny cottage in the hamlet by the Royal Forestry Society in 1983 but is looking rather sickly, another, planted more recently on the hillside by the Malvern Hills Conservators, is protected by a metal fence, but neither seem to have white leaves. The location of the third oak has not yet been identified.

Some local people have also suggested that the Malvern Hills were used as a ritual calendar by the Dobunni, with the sites of White Leaved Oak, Midsummer Hill and British Camp at the southern end of the range, used in Druid spring and summer rituals and burials, whilst the Worcestershire Beacon and northern hills were used for autumn and winter fire festivals, with sacrificial cremations and interments of their dead. As the sun was central to Druid beliefs and worship, the cave that once existed at Ivy

Clutter's Cave on the western slope of British Camp, © Bob Embleton

Arthur's Stone, a Neolithic cromlech in Herefordshire, c3200 BC, ©UKgeofan

Scar Rock in the north-east and Clutters Cave in the south-west, were also said to have been used to observe the rising and setting sun respectively, particularly on the two equinoxes. Then the sun emerges over the Bambury Stone on Bredon Hill in the east and sets over Arthur's Stone, a Neolithic cromlech in the west, on the ridge line of a hill in Herefordshire, which overlooks both the Golden and the Wye Valleys.

On the hillside directly below Clutters Cave on the side of British Camp, is a large stone, said to have fallen from the cave entrance, which from its smooth shape has long been claimed to have been used for Druidic human sacrifice. Other people claim that the four by six foot cave was originally a large volcanic bubble formed beneath the Silurian Sea, which was only hollowed out further by man, probably to be used as an ancient hermitage, although it has never been dated. Another ancient local legend recalls that the tiny Clutters Cave or *"Clutters Bower"*, used to be known as *"the Giants Cave"*, whose occupant, in a fit of anger at his wife's infidelity, killed her by throwing an entrance stone down onto her in Colwall, where it remained at the crossroads for many centuries. Yet another story says that two giants agreed to throw the stone from the hills and that where it fell should be the boundary between their lands. Across Britain tales of men called *"giants"* are often associated with ancient pre-Celtic sites. Even as late as the 17th century one Worcestershire man, tall enough to be known as a giant, lived at Ripple. The gravestone of Robert Reeve recorded that he was seven feet four inches tall and died aged fifty-six in 1626, after *"mowing an acre of land in one day in Uckingshall meadow"*. *(Notes and Queries for Worcestershire, by John Noake, 1856)* The Colwall Stone still rests at the central road junction in the village, but is now claimed by some to be an 18th century replacement of the original.

However, the Dobunni are known to have been one of the few Celtic tribes to have issued gold and silver coins before the Roman invasion. At first these may have been used as a gift exchange between tribes, to denote loyalty or to pay tribute to other chiefs. These coins could then be melted down by their recipients to make jewellery and other precious objects, rather than being used for buying and selling goods. Most have the distinctive motif of a three-tailed horse on one side and on the reverse either a stylised head, probably representing a leader, or an ear of wheat symbolising the fertility of their land and tribe.

Celtic style head and three tailed horse on a silver Dubonnic coin from c70 BC

38

For the most part each area had a local male or female Druid leader, who we might recognise as a magistrate, legislator, priest or chieftain. Tacitus wrote *"In Britain, there is no rule of distinction to exclude the female line from the throne, or the command of armies"*. Women were merely household chattels in ancient Greece, whilst in Rome the role of women was still very restricted in comparison to the Celts. In Britannia and Galatia, whether married or single, women owned their own property, and women such as Eponina, Onomaris, Cartismandua and most famously Boudicca, became tribal rulers, oracles, powerful Druid priestesses or warrior leaders. In about 60 AD, after her daughters were raped by Roman invaders, Boudicca, Queen of the Iceni tribe in Essex, led her warrior army to destroy the Roman town of Colchester, followed by burning Londinium (London) to the ground.

Celtic sagas are peopled with women of power, but the early Christian

writers regarded such strong females in Celtic history as sorceresses, and relegated them to the roles of *"witches"* or *"fairy women"*. After the establishment of Christianity the Celts were forgotten for centuries, and the histories of their Roman conquerors, by writers such as Caesar, Plato and Tacitus, were only rediscovered during the early Renaissance, including the tale of Boudicca, Buddug, or Boadicea. Later, the Victorians romanticised her story, making parallels between this heroic woman leader in Ancient Britain and their own Queen.

'Boadicea haranguing the Britons', by John Opie, 19th century

But back in the Midlands, during the first century AD, the whole Dubonnic territory was divided between two male rulers or 'kings', Corio in the south-west and Bodvoc in the north-east. These rulers may also have had overlords from the neighbouring Catuvellauni tribe in the south whose 'king' was Caradoc, or Caractacus, his Latin name. With his brother Togodomus, Caractacus had led the initial British resistance against the Roman invasion commanded by Aulus Plautius in 43 AD. But the Catuvellauni were driven back and Togodomus was killed in the battle of the Thames. Caractacus moved his fighters north into part of the territory of the Dobunni, but their leader Bodvoc was reluctant to join him in warfare against the Legionaries. Before the Romans had even reached his territory, Bodvoc had conceded to the invading soldiers of

Plautius. Caractacus is thought to have then taken shelter with Corio and the remaining anti-Roman section of the Dobunni in about 47 AD, possibly moving onto the Malvern Hills for protection and further fortifying British Camp, but there is no evidence of any military engagement here. Then, whilst Bodvoc and the north-eastern Dobunni were rapidly adopting a Romano-British lifestyle, Caractacus moved his warriors further north to join the Silures living in South Wales. The Roman soldiers then bypassed the Malverns as they pushed onwards into the Silurian territories.

'Bodvoc's Stone', commemorative pillar from Margam Mountain, South Wales

The Silures were quite unlike their more peaceable southern neighbours and led by Caractacus from about 48 AD, they fought fiercely against those Legionaries who were trying to build Roman forts across their territory. They were a loose network of groups based to the north of the Severn Estuary, with known Iron Age hill-forts at Sudbrook and Llanmelin, plus roundhouses at Gwehelog and Chepstow. The Silures, meaning *"the dark-haired people"*, were considered to be so dangerous that the Roman legate Ostorius declared they should be *"exterminated or transplanted"*, which only made them fight more strongly.

Some of the ideas of the Reverend Henry Card, a 19th century Vicar of Malvern, are still popular locally. In 1822 he claimed that Caractacus  fought his last battle at British Camp on the Malvern Hills, but this is contradicted by the accounts of the Roman writer Tacitus. Edward Elgar was told about this popular legend of the last stand at the Camp by his mother. He wrote his famous cantata entitled *"Caractacus"* in 1898, whilst living at 'Forli' in Alexandra Road, Malvern. But two centuries after the actual events, Tacitus had provided us with a considerable record of the wars between the Romans and the Britons, including the last battle of Caractacus. Tacitus relates how, after his brother was killed, Caractacus fled north with his warriors to the land of the Silures in South Wales, waging continuous guerrilla attacks against the Roman occupation. But when the Romans moved considerable forces into the Silurian lands, he took his warriors even further north into the land of the Ordivician tribes. Having fought bravely against the Romans for a total of nine years, it seems Caractacus finally faced them in North Wales. Tacitus records the site of the final battle in detail, describing a river flowing directly in front of the hill, quite unlike Malvern's British Camp.

"Caractacus had shifted the war by a stratagem into the territory of the Ordovices, where, joined by all who dreaded peace with us, he resolved on a final struggle. He selected a position for the engagement in which advance and retreat alike would be difficult for our men and comparatively easy for his own, and then on some lofty hills, wherever their sides could be approached by a gentle slope, he piled up stones to serve as a rampart. A river too of varying depth was in his front, and his armed bands were drawn up before his defences." (from the Writings of Tacitus, 2nd century AD - Complete Works of Tacitus, Random House, 1942)

Most historians today believe that Caractacus was defeated in North Wales at the battle of Caer Caradoc, (Fort of Caradoc or Caractacus), but this could be any one of three hill-forts, all of which lack the adjacent river. As there is no conclusive archaeological evidence, the actual site of his final stand is still unidentified. His wife, sons and daughter were all captured at the fort, along with his other brothers, although Caractacus escaped, seeking refuge with Cartismandua, Queen of the Brigantes, his step-mother. He was betrayed and handed over in chains by the Queen and her husband, Venutius, who was loyal to the Emperor. But perhaps the Queen had not approved this action, as she is said to have soon divorced Venutius and married his charioteer.

Meanwhile, the entire family of Caractacus was taken back to Rome as captives in 51 AD. *"Then came a procession of the royal vassals, and the ornaments and neck-chains and the spoils which Caractacus had won in wars with other tribes, were displayed. Next were to be seen his brothers, his wife and daughter; last of all, Caractacus himself. All the rest stooped in fear and abject supplication; not so the king, who neither by humble look nor speech sought compassion. When he was set before the emperor's tribunal, he spoke as follows: "My present lot is as glorious to you as it is degrading to myself. I had men and horses, arms and wealth, which I parted with reluctantly. If you Romans choose to lord it over the world, does it follow that the world is to accept slavery? Were I to have been immediately delivered up as a prisoner, neither my fall nor your triumph would have become famous. My punishment would have been followed by oblivion, whereas, if you now save my life, I shall be an everlasting memorial of your clemency." Upon this the emperor granted pardon to Caractacus, to his wife, and to his brothers and they were released from their bonds." (from the Writings of Tacitus, 2ⁿᵈ century AD -*

Complete Works of Tacitus. Random House, 1942)

Caractacus at the Tribunal of Claudius, by Andrew Birrell after Fuseli, 1792

Revered as a brave warrior and leader, the Romans treated Caractacus as an honoured celebrity. His sister Gladys is believed to have taken the Roman name Claudia on her marriage to a Patrician, Rufus Pudens. The sons and daughter of Caractacus are thought to have already been Christians when they arrived in Italy, whilst his aged father Bran, who had come on the journey as a voluntary hostage, was still an Arch-Druid. Bran is claimed by some to have been baptised in Rome in 58 AD by Saint Paul, and that when the family returned to the Silurian lands in South Wales they supported the e a r l y Christian missionaries arriving from Europe. Caractacus died in Rome in 54 AD, having outlived the Roman general Ostorius who had captured him. The Roman armies eventually left Britain in 410 AD, after 350 years of occupation, and much of the population of Britannia then returned to their pagan beliefs and ceremonies.

Druid worship as visualised by E. Walcousins, 19ᵗʰ century

Carving of a severed head in a basket with a distended tongue and bulging eyes.
Hand-rest of a medieval monk's seat in Little Malvern Priory

Chapter III

Missionaries, Monks and Martyrs

Repeated Norse invasions by small bands of warriors now led to Saxon migration into this country along with Angles, Jutes, and Frisians, around the time of the collapse of Roman authority. The Saxons invaded the Severn valley, defeating the local Britons by 577. They gradually settled on homesteads in new clearings within the forests, giving us many of the Anglo-Saxon place names for present villages and parishes. But they then founded rival Saxon kingdoms that fought each other and under their subsequent Saxon Kings, including Offa of Mercia in the Midlands, Ethelbert of Kent and Ine of Wessex, the country continued to be turbulent.

One vivid account of the take-over of southern Britannia by the Saxons came from a native Briton, Gildas, who lived at that time. *"All the columns were leveled with the ground by the frequent strokes of the battering-ram, all the husbandmen routed, together with their priests, bishops and people, whilst the swords gleamed and the flames crackled around them on every side. Lamentable to behold, in the midst of the streets lay the tops of lofty towers, tumbled to the ground, stones of high walls, holy altars, fragments of human bodies, covered with livid clots of coagulated blood, looking as if they had been squeezed together in a press; and with no chance of being buried, save in the ruins of the houses, or in the ravening bellies of wild beasts and birds."*

Anglo Saxon Sutton-Hoo helmet, British Museum
© *Mike Markowski*

Life became more peaceable after the conversion of Ethelbert of Kent to Christianity in 597 and recovery gradually followed. Ancient sacred sites such as Celtic wells were often contained within the first modest Saxon

44

churches, w ith Christian baptism, marriage and funeral rituals superseding traditional pagan rites of passage. Gradually the previous British customs and social responsibilities were acknowledged and recorded as ancient laws, written down by Wilfred of York in the 670s. This bonded the Saxon Kings with their Celtic subjects, bringing stability to the country. In 672, a council of the English Church was held at Worcester. In 680 a church was built here and Bosel, a monk from Whitby, was appointed as the first bishop, creating the new diocese of Worcester in the Hwiccan sub-kingdom of Mercia. The Saxon Abbey at Pershore was founded in 689. Eventually under Alfred the Great, a Saxon born in present day Oxfordshire, most of the country became unified into the kingdom of England by 897 in the face of the Viking invasions.

Ancient stone head and shoulders now in St Anne's Chapel, Malvern Priory

Famous 'Lustyman' figure on Boa Island, County Fermanagh, 400 to 800 AD
courtesy of Paul Lavery, the Ulster Card Company

At Malvern an ancient carved head and shoulders, probably from this early period, was excavated from the Priory grounds and can be found in

St Anne's Chapel. Although little is known about this primitive stone carving, it is similar to one of the two pagan figures now in the Christian graveyard of Caldragh, Boa Island, Ireland, which are believed to date from before the 8th century. Also within the Malvern Priory precinct, "*A celt, (axe-like chisel) of a metal apparently between brass and copper, about five inches long, with a beautiful patina, and a small ring, was found here, at a considerable depth below the surface of the ground, about the middle of the last century*". *(Topographical Dictionary of England by Samuel Lewis, 1831)* These finds suggest the Priory site may have even earlier sacred origins.

Before the 11th century the hills above the marshy *"wilderness"* of Malvern's forests were sparsely inhabited by solitary Christian hermits, who had renounced all worldly goods to live alone beside the spring water sources. Legend has it that one hermit lived in "Clutters Cave" above Walm's Well, possibly another by the spring on Westminster Bank in West Malvern, near the site of a cottage now called *"The Hermitage"*, in an area later owned by the Abbey of Westminster. A third hermit was said to have inhabited *"The Devil's Pulpit"*, a cave long since collapsed, at Ivy Scar Rock near North Hill spring .*"Before the conquest, Malvern was a wilderness, thick set with trees, in the midst of which some monks who aspired to greater perfection, retired thither from the priory of Worcester, and became hermits."* *(History of Worcestershire, Dr T. Nash, 1781)*

Like Christ living in the desert wilderness, hermits considered life here *"in the wild foreste"* to be a real test of their faith. At that time superstition and fear surrounded the unforeseen dangers of *"mountains"*, *"wilderness"*, *"witchcraft"*, and *"wild beasts"*, including wild boar and of course wolves. Some of these dangers were real enough. It was later recorded that in the hills of Mathon, near today's Brockhill Road in West Malvern, Farley Park was newly created in 1250 and well stocked with deer, but by 1287 these had all been destroyed by wolves. Numbers of Worcestershire men earned their living as professional *"wolf-hunters"* in the county before wolves were completely eradicated in England in 1509.

Onuphrius, a 4th century Christian hermit who lived in the Egyptian desert

In the 15th century it was claimed that another Malvern hermit, a monk called Werstan, apparently lived in these wild woods, firstly in the small cave in Holly Mount Wood, still in the grounds of Holly Mount House in Great Malvern. After visiting the monks at Malvern Priory in 1523, John Leland wrote about Werstan, saying that when the monastery at Deerhurst had been *"destroyed by the Danes. Werstanus fledde thens, as it is sayde, to Malverne"*. This Viking invasion came from the nearby river Severn, forcing Werstan to flee eighteen miles through the marshy woods to try to seek safety on the Malvern Hills. In the early 1060s he was *"guided by angels"* to build a little oratory here, a tiny chapel to St Michael, where he was later martyred.

'Wolf' head in the 8th century Saxon church, the Priory of St Mary, formerly an Abbey, beside the original site of the Deerhurst monastery "destroyed by Danes"

According to Jabez Allies in *"The Antiquities and Folklore of Worcestershire"*, these Viking invaders sometimes also met a grisly end. *"The hapless Dane who fell into the hands of the citizens of Worcester on any of his marauding excursions, was flayed alive and his tanned hide affixed to the cathedral doors as a terrible warning to his countrymen."* One young Dane, who tried to steal the silver *"Compline Bell"* from Worcester's Saxon Cathedral, was caught and flayed alive. During the night the monks threw his body, still living, onto the deck of his invading Viking ship on the Severn, which hurriedly departed. In the 19th century the leather, still covering part of the Cathedral's doors, was identified as human skin and a small remnant of it was then kept in a glass case in the Cathedral.

Following the Norman Conquest, by 1083 Benedictine monks had established the monastery at Great Malvern, the Priory Church in 1085 and Little Malvern Priory in 1127, relying on the springs for their domestic water supplies. But it seems that the first ever portrayal of the legend of *"Abbot"* Werstan was not until 1465, in the new stained glass windows of the refurbished Malvern Priory and after this it became inaccurately known as *"The Abbey"*. Here he can still be seen founding the little oratory of St Michael with the help of angels, then as *"Holy Werstan"* being martyred by a swordsman striking at his head as he leans out of the chapel window. But Leland is careful to qualify his report of 'Abbot' Werstan with the phrase *"it is said"*, indicating that there may be some factual doubts about this story. As no earlier written records of Werstan have yet been

Drawing of the martyrdom of Werstan from the Priory window, 1465

found and no such martyr or saint appears in the Christian calendar, some historians have questioned both his martyrdom and even his existence.

The Priory Church was built on the north side of the monastery cloisters, but at least twenty years before its foundation in 1085, the monks' little hermitage of St Michael was recorded as existing on the slope of the hill above. *"Great Malvern was a place of great antiquity; for here in the wild forest, was an hermitage or some kind of religious house for seculars, before the conquest (1066), endowed by the gift of Edward the Confessor, as is stated more than once in the charter of King Henry I, recorded in about 1083."(John Chambers, A General History of Malvern, 1817)*

In 1544 Richard, Robert and Roger Taverner were noted as buying *"Saint Myghelles chapel, with its garden, beneath le Malvern Hyll"* and some early maps also record this early religious building at the foot of the Worcestershire Beacon. It was marked on a plan of Great Malvern in

48

1725 by Joseph Dougherty and was again recorded as St Michael's Hermitage, a small right angle building, on his map of 1744.

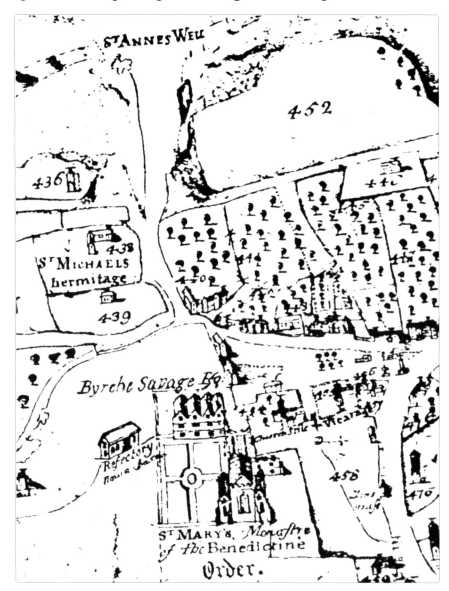

Map of the village of Malvern in 1744, showing St Michael's hermitage

The little building was on a narrow terrace between the Hay Well and St Ann's Well, above today's Rose Bank Gardens in the vicinity of Foley Terrace. Eighty years later when a cottage called *"the Hermitage"* was demolished on this site, a small crypt containing many encaustic tiles was found, like those from the 15th century in the present Priory. *"That there was a chapel dedicated to St Michael, with a residence for some seculars, on the site where a small cottage now stands, in which a Mr Banister now resides, appears evident as the cottage is erected on part of the walls of the chapel. In many places of this cottage are the same kind of curiously inscribed tiles as those which formed part of the pavement of the ancient church. Very many of the same kind of tiles have been frequently dug up out of that part converted into a garden. ... It is equally evident that the*

The 'Abbey Gateway' in 1731, possibly showing the hermitage on the hill above

orchard belonging to the same cottage was a burial ground, from coffin furniture and bones which are constantly found when it is ploughed up. ... As a further proof that it was a cell or hermitage for anchorites, the ancient writings of the house refer to it as 'The Hermitage', by which name it is still known." (Mary Southall, A Description of Malvern, 1825) Several 18th century engravings of the *"Abbey Gateway"* show a small building on the hill slope in the background, possibly the hermitage.

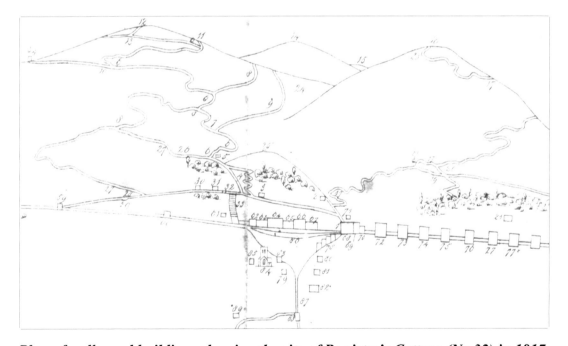

Plan of walks and buildings showing the site of Banister's Cottage (No.32) in 1817

It seems that the later 15th century Malvern monks had promoted *"Holy Werstan the Martyr"* to enhance the pedigree and importance of their monastery and refurbished Priory Church. Perhaps at the same date they also renovated St Michael's oratory, embellishing it with their newly made tiles. Today the site is thought to be under the house named *"Bello*

50

*The Ninety-Nine Steps, with
Bello Sguardo at the top, c1900*

Sguardo" at the top of the Ninety-Nine Steps. Beside the house there was an old donkey stable dating from the 1820s, but now two modern garages have been built there. In the 1970s the owner, Phillip Evans, took up the stable floor and found two early unmarked stone slabs which he put in the garden. Mr Evans described these as *"coffin lids"* and as his spade often hit other solid flat surfaces in the garden, he suggested that the area could have been a graveyard for the monks and might have other burials in it.

But another young hermit, *"an unlettered man"* named Alwin, Adwin or Aldwin, also stayed for some time in the isolation of the wilderness of Malvern. Perhaps Aldwin was drawn to the little oratory of St Michael, to live as a novice in the adjoining *"hermitage for anchorites"* at about the time of the attack on Werstan. Later, after becoming a monk, Aldwin decided to accompany a man called Guy or Guido, possibly a Viking, who sought to do penance by

going on a pilgrimage to the Holy Land. Nott suggests that this was because they both, or at least Guido, felt some guilt about the murder of Werstan. *"Guido, supposed to be a Dane, and perchance in some way implicated in St. Werstan's murder and Aldwyn, residents of this neighbourhood, a little before the time of the Conquest determined, for some reason, and perhaps because of their sin in the Saint's martyrdom, to become palmers, and visit the*

*Novices at the hermitage being beaten by
Danes with switches, Priory window, 1465*

Lord's Sepulchre at Jerusalem, or meet with a glorious death at the hands of the Saracens." (Antiquities of 'Moche' Malvern, by James Nott, 1885) (*"Palmers"* were pilgrims returning from Jerusalem with palm fronds as holy souvenirs.)

Aldwin travelled to Worcester to ask his Saxon Bishop, Wulfstan, for permission to make this pilgrimage. But Wulfstan, (later St Wulstan), refused Aldwin's request, predicting that through him *"God would work great things in Malvern"*. It seems Guido departed, but Aldwin obediently returned to the Malvern Hills and, over about seventeen years, gradually attracted thirty other monks to join him. *"They agreed to live under the order of St Benedict, and elected Alwin one of their company to be Superior."* (Dr T. Nash, History of Worcestershire, 1799)

In the 6th century, before becoming a monk, St Benedict had been a devout and disciplined French hermit, who had devised a strict routine of work and prayer, soon adopted by others in Europe. Following his example, the brotherhood in *"Moche"* Malvern became an organised religious community, Aldwin founding the Benedictine monastery by 1083, supplied with water piped from the nearby Hay Spring. About two years later, in 1085 Aldwin founded the adjoining Priory Church, daughter church to the Abbey of Westminster. At first the new church was dedicated to St Mary but later also to St Michael, perhaps in memory of Werstan and the earlier little oratory. Aldwin is recorded as dying in 1140, when he would have been about ninety-five years old, but as his successor as prior died in 1135, this is thought by some to be improbable.

The damaged lid of the tomb of this second prior, *"Doctor Walcherus"*,

was excavated from the grounds beside the south side of the Priory in 1711, where it had probably been thrown during the destruction of the monastery cloisters under Henry VIII. Now in St Anne's Chapel, the Latin inscription re-cut on this stone slab, tells us that he was skilled as a philosopher, astrologer, geometrician and mathematician. This French intellectual, born in the Dukedom of Lorraine, came to England in about 1091, after the Norman Conquest. He was famed for using an astrolabe from the Middle East to measure the time of several solar and lunar eclipses across Europe, within an accuracy of about fifteen minutes. To replace the more complex Roman numerals used at that time, he also introduced the Arabic numbers we use today. But sadly no physical evidence of the first Prior, Aldwin, has ever been found. Perhaps his tomb still lies undiscovered in the grounds of the little lost chapel of St Michael, somewhere on the hillside above.

52

Knights Templar defeated in 1187 at the Battle of Hattin, now in Israel. Miniature from a medieval manuscript c1490, Bibliothèque Nationale, France

Chapter IV

Knights Templar in Much Malvern

Although Aldwin wasn't able to make a pilgrimage to Jerusalem, other Benedictine monks from the Malvern monastery may well have done so. The first Crusade was launched in 1095 by Pope Urban II, only ten years after the founding of the Malvern Priory Church. The following year 100,000 mostly ordinary men, women, children and monks flocked to the Holy Land, both as pilgrims seeking absolution from their sins and as fighters known as *"the People's Army"*. One man buried inside the Priory Church by the late 12th century, was said not only to have been a Crusader but also a Knight Templar. Originally his tomb was sited against the south wall, but over the centuries his stone effigy was moved to several other locations around the church and became very damaged. At some point his feet, resting on a small dog, were broken off and lost, only to be rediscovered in 1839 when the new wall of the south transept was being constructed. *"In a recess is a monument of unquestionable antiquity; it is a mutilated statue of a knight. ... It is supposed to represent Walter Corbet, Templar, arrayed in mail armour of the Conqueror's time, having a long surcoat over it. The right hand is armed with a battle-axe; the left holds a circular shield or target, and from under it hangs a sword." (Mary Southall, A Description of Malvern, 1825)*

Engraving of the knight's effigy in Malvern Priory before his feet had been found

The whole figure can still be seen today, now raised up on a simple plinth to the left of the main altar. He is dressed in chain-mail, but unusually, rather than a sword in his right hand, he holds *"a halbert like a pickaxe" (Stukeley's Itinery, 18ᵗʰ century),* making this rare sculpture of a Templar, earlier in date than some of the nine effigies in the London Temple.

Head of the unknown 12ᵗʰ century Knight Templar in Great Malvern Priory

The Corbets were an important Shropshire family and, amongst many others, gave great material assistance to the Benedictine monks of Malvern so that they *"were enabled to raise, endow, and beautify their church and monastery." (Mary Southall, A Description of Malvern, 1825)* One later monument in the Priory, probably dating from the 15ᵗʰ century, was to another Corbet, Richard, also a Knight, but this was *"a very plain table monument without any ornaments whatever; the sides and ends of the tomb covered with tiles, five inches and a half square, of a red and yellow colour, like the others with the armorial bearings." (Malvern Priory Church by James Nott, 1895)*

It has also been suggested that the carved effigy could be from the tomb of Brian de Brompton, another generous Knight Templar, patron and almsgiver to the Priory who died in the 13ᵗʰ century. In his will of 1262 he asked to be buried in the Priory *"along with his horses and other belongings"*, but the old style of the chain-mail on the anonymous effigy suggest it dates from at least one hundred years earlier. Possibly the sculpture represents William Burdet of Alvecote, a Knight who had returned home from the Crusades during that earlier period. In 1159 he donated enough of his lands to the Malvern Priory for the building of a monastery in Warwickshire, although it's believed that no more than five monks ever took up residence there. A tragic local tale tells how, at his homecoming a few years earlier, a trusted servant told William that his wife had been unfaithful while he was away. The enraged Knight immediately stabbed her to death, only to discover that the steward had been lying to cover up his own dishonesty. So William's generous gift to the Priory was actually his remorseful penance for the brutal murder of his wife, in the hope of absolution from this mortal sin, making him a less likely candidate for a prominent memorial. So despite these records of several

possible Templar burials here, the true identity of the Knight's effigy in the Priory still remains a mystery.

Mystery and myth also surround the activities of the Knights Templar, who were originally only a small group of French Benedictine monks, monastic knights who went to fight in the Holy Land. The first Crusade ended in 1099 with the Christian occupation of Jerusalem, but pilgrims on their journeys through the countryside still suffered regular attacks, both from robbers and the Saracens. At first only nine brothers of the Benedictine order came together in 1118 to officially protect the pilgrims and their routes, although they had probably already been doing this for some years. Originally dedicated to *"poverty, chastity and obedience"*, these few impoverished monastic knights and their horses were given

quarters by the King of Jerusalem, Baldwin II, in his palace on the Temple Mount on the site of the Temple of Solomon, so they became known as the Knights Templar. From 1128 they were governed by a strict moral code adapted from the Cistercians and in 1139 were formally recognised as a monastic military order by the Pope.

Seal of the Knights Templar; two knights on a single horse, the symbol of early poverty

The order attracted many other monastic brothers to join them and fought strongly throughout the Crusades for the next 200 years. They often wore a surcoat over their chain mail to identify themselves; a white tabard with a red cross, the symbol both of Christ and St George the dragon-slayer, which later became the flag of England. They gradually gained wealth, lands and power, extending their influence beyond the religious wars in the Middle East into European

An early Knight Templar in the Holy Land

politics and banking. As the order had taken many precious religious relics and treasures into their protection, said to have included the Ark of the Covenant, the Holy Grail and the Turin Shroud, they became very secretive about the places where these valuables were stored. Under strict rules to ensure security, they employed numerous skilled stonemasons to build fortified monastic castles across Europe and the Holy Land where these treasures could be safely kept. The Knights also invented the equivalent of today's safety deposit boxes for the use of visitors, and travellers' cheques that could be cashed at other Templar buildings, a great boon to both pilgrims and merchant traders on their long journeys. Consequently these disciplined religious men were regarded as very trustworthy, becoming highly discreet bankers for many monarchs, Popes and some Muslim leaders.

The wealth and secrecy of their order eventually attracted accusations of heresy from the impoverished King of France, Phillip IV, and his friend the French Pope Clement V, leading to the arrest of many Knights in 1307. Despite their entreaties of innocence, supported by a further 6,000 Knights Templar, fifty-seven of the most senior members were tried as heretics, tortured and burnt at the stake. Many of the other Knights Templar fled to escape further persecution, often to the remoter parts of Europe. Much of the Templar land and wealth was confiscated and many of their buildings were given to the Knights Hospitallers, who cared for sick pilgrims. Established in the twelfth century, the

Jaques de Molay, Templar Grand Master, burnt at the stake in 1314

Knights Hospitallers ran hospitals in Jerusalem and elsewhere in the Crusader states, institutions which then spread into Europe.

The destruction of the Templar order in England was less violent, although some Knights were suddenly arrested in 1308 and transferred to the Tower of London, York and Lincoln Castles. But only three Knights were forced to confess that they were guilty of heresy. After this their property was confiscated, but they were then absolved and reconciled to the church. A few other Knights Templar were mildly punished, including John de Coningston and six Knights who were sent to different monasteries in Worcestershire to do penance. But the Templars continued to own great amounts of land in the county. *"In Worcestershire, the manor of the Templars at Lawern, and lands in Flavel, Temple Broughton, and Hanbury, ... but it would be tedious further to continue with a dry detail of ancient names and places; sufficient has been said to give an idea of the enormous wealth of the order in this country, where it is known to have possessed some hundreds of manors, the right of presentation to churches innumerable, and thousands of acres of arable land, pasture, and woodland, besides villages, farm-houses, mills, and tithes, rights of common, of fishing, of cutting wood in forests, &c. &c."(Dr T. Nash, History of Worcestershire, 1781)*

In order to avoid arrest, some Knights fled back to Scotland. It has often been claimed that they then founded Freemasonry there as a secret society, with the Rosslyn Chapel built at its heart in 1456, but no direct historical link for this claim has ever been proved. It's thought that much of the apparent Masonic imagery in the chapel was added later when David Bryce, an Edinburgh architect and known Freemason, was commissioned in the 1860s by James St Clair, the third Earl of Rosslyn, to undertake restoration of the church, probably including work on many of the carvings.

Some say that Freemasonry only began to emerge in England in the eighteenth century, with apparent links between the moral legacy of the Knights Templar and the secret traditions of their stonemasons. *"Young men were apprenticed to the stonemasons, (who were formed into 'Lodges') and in due course passed through their training and became 'Free'. Given that they were engaged in the construction of religious edifices, their masters applied a moral code which was taught to them (because they were illiterate) by word of mouth and was illustrated by allegory and symbols." (Malvern Freemasonry and the Masonic Hall, 2005)* These Stonemasons' Lodges then began to admit other influential 'Free' men who were not in their trade but had agreed to abide by their

58

Set-square & compass, insignia of the Freemasons,
© *Nabokov*

traditions and strict codes of moral conduct. These traditions and moral principles are still acted out at Masonic meetings today through ritual and drama, and illustrated symbolically by the working tools of stonemasons, including the compass, set-square and plumb-rule. All members must also profess a belief in a Supreme Being known as *"The Great Architect"*. Their traditional vows threatened to kill any woman who learned Masonic secrets of *"the Craft"*, and women are still excluded from full membership today. For many years Roman Catholics were also excluded from membership and are now forbidden from joining by Papal decree.

But perhaps the very beginning of Freemasonry can be traced back to the 16th century, with connections to the earlier restoration of Malvern Priory completed in about 1460. *"On the 24th June, 1502, a lodge of master-masons was formed at Westminster, at which King Henry VII presided as grand master, having appointed John Islip abbot, and Sir Reginald Bray knight of the garter."* *(Hollingshed – Malvern Priory Church, James Nott, 1895)*

Coat of Arms of the United Lodge of England

Born in St John's, Worcester in 1424, Sir Reginald Bray became a prominent architect, soldier, statesman and master-mason, and one of Henry's closest advisors. The second son of Sir Richard Bray, he was educated at the Royal Grammar School Worcester and having helped Henry gain the throne, was made a Knight of the Bath at his coronation. In 1502 King Henry's new Lady Chapel in Westminster Abbey was being built with Sir Reginald's architectural guidance, a splendid gothic hall, said to be the last great masterpiece of English medieval architecture. Sir Reginald died a year later and having also supervised the building of St George's Chapel at Windsor Castle, he was buried there. But throughout the 1450s Sir Reginald Bray had been the young master-mason, *"skilled in architecture"*, who led the extensive medieval reconstruction of the Malvern Priory Church. This major work included entirely rebuilding *"the presbytery, choir and choir aisles"*, creating *"a new tower, built upon the Norman tower-piers, having necessarily strengthened the older masonry"*, as well as literally raising the roof. By 1465 Sir Reginald had already been immortalised in the Priory's stained glass, where his image can still be seen, third from the left in the lowest section of the north window in the former Jesus Chapel, next to the image of Henry's son, Prince Arthur.

The first known Grand Lodge of Freemasons was formed in England in June 1717. At their early Masonic meetings the all-male membership sometimes wore the now familiar white tabard with a red cross of the Knights Templar. In a recent statement from the Provincial Grand Lodge of Worcestershire, the origins of *"The Order of the Temple, the Knights Templar, and the Order of the Knights of Malta"* were described in some detail. *"There is however, no claim, or indeed evidence, to any historical link between the Masonic Orders and the mediaeval military orders. Each Order has its own distinct ceremonies, and regalia. The earliest records of Masonic Knight Templar activity appear in 1777 when the minutes of some Royal Arch Chapters show that the rituals were being worked as appendant degrees in that Order. ... Whilst it is permissible for a Knight of Malta to attend a Priory of Malta meeting wearing Knight Templar regalia most members of the Order eventually prefer to acquire the appropriate Regalia."*

18th century Masonic Knights Templar

A Masonic Lodge was first founded in Worcester in 1790 and in the following years many Malvern residents became members, playing an influential role in the early development of both the city and the village.

During the eighteenth century in Britain many renowned male luminaries became Freemasons taking vows of *"Brotherly love, Relief* (charity) *and Truth"*. Early Freemasons included Robbie Burns, Sir Isaac Newton, Benjamin Franklin and William Hogarth, and other prominent members in the twentieth century were Sir Winston Churchill, Captain Scott, Oscar Wilde, Sir Alexander Fleming, Rudyard Kipling and King George VI.

Freemason's initiation ceremony c1805, based on engraving by Gabanon of 1745

A *"Masonic Soiree & Exhibition"* opened at the Guildhall in Worcester in August 1884 and became the foundation of today's Masonic Museum and Library at the Masonic Hall, Rainbow Hill, Worcester, which is open to the public. *"No less than 140 exhibitors displayed an array of Masonic artefacts: books and manuscripts, china, glass and pottery, prints and paintings, coins, medals and jewels. The event was organised by the Provincial Grand Secretary, George Taylor, under the auspices of the Provincial Grand Master, Sir Edmund Lechmere, and William Williamson, the Mayor of Worcester."* *(Museum Curator, John Hart, 2009)*

Coat of arms of the Lechmere family in Hanley Castle churchyard

There are now about one hundred and thirty Masonic Lodges in Worcestershire. In Great Malvern itself *"The Royds Lodge"* was founded in 1867. This first Masonic Lodge was consecrated at Townsend House, the water-cure establishment of Dr Ralph Grindrod, followed by a dedication service at Malvern Priory. The Lodge expanded to include many local businessmen, architects, builders, doctors, chemists, historians and councillors, who held great power in the growing town. *"Throughout the years there have been many Freemasons in Malvern who have had notable connections with the local community; local businessmen who have influenced the development of the town or who have risen to high Masonic office."* (Malvern Freemasonry and the Masonic Hall, by W.Bro. R. F. Hall-Jones, 2005) A second lodge was added in Malvern in 1919, *"St Werstan's Lodge,* and in 1934 *"The Royds Royal Arch Chapter"*, which is now one of the largest chapters in the county. After the Second World War in 1949 *"The Malvern Hills Lodge"* was created, followed by *"The Malvern Priory Lodge"* in 1969, and most recently *"The Morgan Lodge"* in 2006. In the 1960s several huge 'conferences' of Freemasons were held in the Malvern Festival Theatre, refurbished and renamed in 1927.

Assembly Rooms and Winter Gardens in 1885, later Malvern Festival Theatre

Today each of Malvern's five current Lodges has about thirty five male members who meet on a regular basis. Since 1912 these meetings have been held in the Masonic Hall on Belle Vue Terrace in the centre of the town and the building is now opened to the public once a year. *"It is not a secret society for almost everything about it can be discussed openly and it is perhaps regrettable that in the past there has been a reluctance to do so. In fact there are*

only a few traditional forms of recognition that masons promise on their honour not to disclose." (Malvern Freemasonry and the Masonic Hall, 2005) It seems that since their endowments to the monastery and Priory of Malvern, the secretive Knights Templar and the later inheritors of their charitable and moral legacy, the Freemasons, have hugely influenced the making and shaping of Great Malvern.

Medieval peasant carrying a bower of May flowers, Malvern Priory miserecord

Chapter V

Feast or Famine in the Forest

alvern was only the name of a large area of sparsely inhabited dense forests, marshes and moorlands in the 11th century, which surrounded the few monastic buildings at the foot of the Malvern Hills, within the lands known as the Chase. In 1066 the now unified and prosperous Anglo-Saxons were defeated in battle by the invading Duke of Normandy, where tradition says King Harold was shot through the eye by an arrow and killed. The new King William I brought the influence of French culture to the royal court, with fashionable nobles and educated inhabitants now adopting French as the official and dominant language in England. This created complex problems of communication, with royal edicts and courtly conversation in French, scholarly books and church services in Latin, while the ordinary population were still speaking in their local Anglo-Saxon dialect.

William 1, Bayeux Tapestry

William, *"the Conqueror"*, spent much of his reign exploring the country, travelling from one manor-house to another but rarely staying for more than two or three days. He met regularly with his Council each Christmas at Gloucester, where he gave the command for the nationwide Doomsday tax survey to take place. Although Malvern was not yet even a hamlet, it was mentioned in the Doomsday Book of 1086 as Malferna, Malveselle and Malveshill. There was also a record of the taxes paid by the occupants of a single dwelling at Baldengate, near today's Barnards' Green. At that time William and his lords probably experienced the good hunting that could be found conveniently nearby in the lands of the Malvern Chase. But perhaps the King had discovered the Chase on an earlier visit in 1066.

A local legend relates that soon after his victory at Hastings, William rode

Site of the Saxon church at Hanley Castle

straight to the Saxon village of Hanley, now Hanley Castle, in the centre of the Malvern Chase, to arrest its Thane, Berthric, Britric or Brihtric Meawe, Lord Snow, (because of his pale flaxen hair), of Tewksbury and Gloucester. William's soldiers arrived and arrested Brihtric on the day Bishop Wulfstan was consecrating the new village church. But earlier in 1045, while on a visit as an envoy to the French Court in Flanders, the wealthy young Brihtric, a descendent of King Ethelred, had unwisely spurned the advances of a love-struck lady, Matilda, daughter of the Earl of Flanders, who later became King William's wife. The story of Matilda's unrequited love appears as a poem in Wace's Chronicle in about 1250, probably copied from an even earlier author. It seems that hell hath no fury…, as even after twenty-one years Matilda apparently had not forgiven or forgotten her humiliation. She now used her influence on the King, who confiscated Brihtric's manor, hall, water mill and lands, throwing him into prison at Winchester where he died miserably, apparently poisoned. The existence of Brihtric is confirmed in the Doomsday survey, which simply records that *"The King holds Hanlie. Brihtric held it."* On her coronation as Queen of England these lands of the Malvern Chase were given to Matilda and only on her death in 1083 was their use for royal hunts claimed by the Crown.

Although much of the Chase remained in the ownership of nobles or the church, it was designated as a *"Royal Forest"* by William, no-longer governed by common law but now by severe 'forest law', specifically designed to protect the deer and other game for the royal hunt. Hunting on horseback with dogs and hawks was central to the lives not only of lords but also many noble ladies, who participated fully and were often as expert as the men. Falconry was regarded as a noble art and the trained hawks were proudly housed in the nobleman's living quarters along with the hounds. The boundaries of the Forest varied through time, but initially stretched from these newly aquired royal hunting quarters at Hanley, to the river Severn at Upton bridge in the east, to the Malvern Hills in the west, from the river Teme at Powick in the north, to Corse Forest in the south. Generally throughout the centuries, whilst under any monarch's direct control these lands became 'the Forest', but whenever the areas were given to nobles they were again called 'the Chase'.

From 1083 onwards a succession of Norman monarchs, their lords or noble relatives reserved the right to use these lands not only to provide the thrill of the chase, but also all the wild ingredients for truly royal feasts. *"In the days of the De Clares and the Beauchamps, Malvern Chase was the home of the wild boar, the stag, the hare and the coney, while many birds and squirrels found shelter in the great trees and masses of foliage which stretched away for miles."* (Hanley Castle by W.S. Symonds, 1883) Under French influence, dining in a noble household had become a great source of pride and pleasure, which now involved many servants in elaborate preparations, both of the food and the table. The well-mannered guests washed ceremonially before and after each feast, eating with their fingers from *"trenchers"*, plates made of coarse bread to soak up the gravy juices, which were then distributed to the poor. A *"trencherman"* was an uncouth guest, greedy enough to eat his 'plate'.

Feast from 'The Very Rich Hours of the Duke of Berry', Musée Condé, France

As well as supplying deer, wild boar, rabbits or *"coneys"*, game birds, and fish from local waterways, the Forest was also a source of wild fruits, nuts, berries, herbs and honey for the aristocratic table. Of course one of the most valuable products of the Forest was timber, providing generous supplies of felled wood for cooking and heating. But much of the timber was also traded for salt and used for firing the Droitwich brine pits where the salt was extracted by evaporation. Salt was essential for curing the perishable meat from the hunt, enabling it to be stored, whereas honey, regarded as an aphrodisiac, was used to sweeten wine and preserve fruits.

But life could be harsh for those lower down the new feudal hierarchy, which stretched from the Norman King 'appointed by God', to barons, earls and knights of the shire who made up the gentry, then to the peasantry at the bottom, comprised of villeins and serfs who were their lord's property and virtually slaves. Hunting in the Malvern Forest without a royal warrant was forbidden and any inhabitants over twelve years of age had to swear an oath *"to be of good behaviour towards his Majesty's wild beasts"*. Foresters were appointed to enforce the law, at first based in Hanley, with the power to sentence most offenders to substantial fines in their court. Poaching was not treated leniently and whether lords or peasants, if caught the culprits were imprisoned until the rich paid very large fines, or the poor had their few assets confiscated. Some nobles just continued hunting as usual and were regularly fined; most prominent offenders were the Beauchamp family and their retainers. In times of real hunger many others became desperate enough not to be deterred by these punishments and it seems that the very poorest, who often *"stole by finding"* a dead or injured deer, were then usually let off. But the worst cases of robbery or murder were heard by travelling Justices who could condemn the culprits to death by beheading at *"Sewet Oaks"* or Sweet Oaks, probably near Hangman's Lane at Blackmore Park. The bodies were then taken up the Pixie Path to the Wyche Pass where they were hung on *"the Forest Gallows"* as a warning to others.

As the poorest inhabitants of the Forest were no longer allowed to catch wild animals for food, they could not survive easily in the district. These peasants rarely ate meat, but lived mainly on a meagre diet of broth, porridge and bread, made from barley, oats or wheat. *"If a deer was found killed, an inquest as to the cause of death was held. The flesh was afterwards given to the nearest hospital, or to the poor and lame of the neighbourhood."* But this only applied to meat from *"those deer that are not sweete, nor meete to be eaten of the best sort of people."* *(Worcestershire Relics, John Noake, 1877)* Consequently the hungry now relied mainly on the charity of the monks to provide for their daily needs and a community of the poor gradually collected around *"Moche"* Malvern Priory, creating a tiny hamlet.

The density of the surrounding woodlands was essential to provide cover for the survival of the deer and wild game, so the felling of trees was also strictly controlled. Some landowners paid substantial fees for licences from the Crown to clear the trees from defined areas of land for the cultivation of wheat, barley or oats, or for keeping herds of pigs, sheep or cattle. *"Great Malvern Priory, for instance, was granted the woods at Baldenhall, Newland, and Woodsfield and was able to clear these without prejudice to the Chase."* (Brian Smith, A History of Malvern, 1964) As more peasants could now work on these pioneer farms, surviving better on the food produced there, the local population gradually increased. The process of licensed clearances was called *"assarting"*, leaving us with Assarts Lane in Malvern Wells. But the work had to be carried out in such a way that it did no harm to the royal hunting preserves. Consequently any new boundary fence or hedge around an assart had to be low enough not to restrict access by the wild animals of the Forest, even though this meant that they could then invade the fields to eat the crops. Such incidents had to be reported to the Forester who would then send keepers to drive them off; *"He hath with his hounds hunted 40 deer of a herd at a time out of the owners' corn and lands"*. As this process caused delays, owners often resorted to chasing deer off with their own dogs. But the Forester would regularly have these dogs *"hombled"* by amputating their front toes and claws so that they could no longer harm the deer, and he could impose harsh fines if this was not done.

In compensation for such damage the inhabitants were given some common rights, which allowed them to collect windfall wood for domestic use only, to turn loose their horses and plough-oxen at night if they wore warning bells, and to release their swine into the woods to fatten up on acorns during the autumn, before rounding them up for winter slaughter. To develop their own trades some residents began to purchase by-products such as fallen timber or animal skins, establishing small local businesses in the Forest and the beginnings of a middle-class. With a good supply of firewood, clay and water, early manufacturers included potters, brick makers, charcoal makers, bakers and tanners, who preserved the animal hides in pits of water and crushed oak bark to make leather; hence Tan House Lane in Upper Howsell. Calf skin was also cured for use as vellum, to be written on by the monks with black ink made from oak gall. The village of *"Much"* Malvern was becoming established. By the 13th century, although the occasional *"villein"* in the Midlands was still sold by his lord like a slave, some peasants were now allowed to rent manorial land to farm as tenants, returning to their masters only to help at peak times of harvesting and ploughing. Others were often released completely from their *"villeinage"* by Malvern Priory or the Bishop of Worcester, if they were to be ordained as monks.

A peasant warming his feet while cooking. Drawing of a Medieval miserecord carving beneath a seat for monks in Worcester Cathedral

In 1778 Nash published an old song with sixteen verses, thought to have been written in about 1590 by the parish clerk, or vicar. This provides one of the earliest records of the natural assets of Much Malvern, including its timber, wild game and pure water, which enabled people to live here.

"That thy prospect is good,
None can deny thee;
Thou hast a great store of wood
Growing hard by thee:
Which is a blessing great
To roast and boil thy meat;
And thee in cold to heat:
    O praise the Lord

A chase for royal deer
Round doth beset thee;
Too many do I fear
For aught they get thee;
Yet tho' they eat away,
Thy corn, thy grass, and hay,
Do not forget, I say,
    To praise the Lord

That noble chase doth give
Thy beasts their feeding;
Where they in summer live
With little heeding;
Thy sheep and swine there go,
So doth thy horse also,
Till winter brings in snow;
       Then praise the Lord

Out of that famous hill
There daily springeth
A water, passing still,
Which always bringeth
Great comfort to all them
That are diseased men,
And makes them well again,
       To praise the Lord"

Motte and bailey castle thought to be of similar design to the castle at Hanley

To better govern the growing population in the Forest from about 1207 'bad' King John began building a castle at Hanley, which served mainly as a hunting lodge. King John always retained a fondness for the county of Worcester, but only stayed at the castle in July 1209 and November 1213, and between these years the Forest assizes were held here. In his historical novel of 1883, W.S. Symonds, Rector of Pendock, created an image of Hanley Castle, *"its great moat filled with fishes, its keep in which we lived, the shattered turrets which formed the angles, and the connecting galleries now very overgrown with ivy and polypody, tower cress, and pennywort." (Hanley Castle by W.S. Symonds, 1883)*

King John hunting in a Forest, c1200

John had always been overshadowed by his popular older brother King Richard, *"the Lionheart"*. While Richard was away on the Third Crusade in 1191, John, in league with Phillip IV of France, had tried to seize the crown. In 1194 Richard returned to England and forgave his brother, but only five years later John did become King when Richard was killed and buried in France, where he had been born.

Unlike his brother, John was always rather unpopular, particularly when he quarrelled with the Pope, who then excommunicated him, invalidating any further christenings or marriages in the kingdom. This placed a great strain on England's Roman Catholic population, who believed that those who remained un-christened and any children born out of wedlock were doomed to hell. Eventually England's powerful Barons rebelled and through William Marshall, a Knight Templar, negotiations at the round Temple Church in London forced John to sign the Magna Carta at Runnymede in 1215, which gave enduring rights to the people of England. Throughout this war John suffered from dysentery and became very ill. When taking a shortcut across the Wash in Lincolnshire, the tide rose faster than expected and his baggage train, containing the crown jewels and royal treasure, was engulfed and lost, so he could no longer pay his soldiers. John rested to make his will and the codicil is still kept in the Worcester Cathedral library. He directed that his body should be buried here, between the effigies of St Oswald and St Wulstan.

King John's 13th century effigy on the 16th century tomb in Worcester Cathedral

Just a few days later in 1216, John died at Newark Castle and as he had wished was buried inside Worcester Cathedral in the beautiful tomb that exists there today, in front of the High Altar. The original 13th century internal coffin is made of hard white Highley stone from Worcestershire, but the present ornamental outer base dates from the 16th century. The lid, carved from Purbeck marble, is believed to be the earliest royal effigy in England. The dark stone was originally painted, the clothing coloured yellow, green and crimson with gold details. When the tomb was opened over five hundred years later, his embalmed body and sword were found in exactly the same position as his effigy above them, but his head was swathed in a monk's cowl.

Portrait of King John on the lid of the tomb, about 1217

The very first Saxon cathedral on this site was superseded by a second cathedral built in 983 by St Oswald, which formed part of the Benedictine Abbey that he also founded. Bishop Wulfstan began building the present cathedral in 1084 and it was completed in 1089. The monastery was dissolved in 1540 by Henry VIII, but much of King John's tomb survived and was soon restored and embellished.

His castle at Hanley also survived until the early sixteenth century, but was no more than a derelict ruin when eventually the parish was sold by Henry VIII. The last remnant of the castle, one crumbling corner tower, was demolished in the late 18th century and the stone was used to rebuild the bridge at Upton, later swept away by floods. At about the same time, quantities of ancient weapons and armour were dredged from the moat and sold as scrap iron. Only the castle mound and remains of the moat can be found today, along the path at the rear of the Hanley Church.

A mourner carved on the side of a destroyed medieval tomb in Little Malvern Priory

Chapter VI

Death, Disease and Survival

Although it relied heavily on rents, revenues, gifts of land and of animals, the Malvern monastery was fairly productive in food for the poor and sick, the monks and visitors. As well as farming *"Malvern Field"* to the north of the Priory and *"South Field"* in the area of today's Abbey Road, by the 13th century they also had a large apple orchard beside Hay Pool and Hay Well, with cider-apple, pear and plum orchards, and probably a vineyard, nearby. Cider, ale and wine could be made locally, often then spiced and mixed with honey to drink.

"Their gardens abounded with fruit trees, herbs for salves, some kinds of cabbage, beans and pot herbs." The monks used the spring waters to cultivate several smaller gardens beside the monastery, including the *"Priors' Garden"*, the *"Cooks' Garden"*, where they grew their vegetables, and the *"Infirmary Garden"* which provided herbs for medicinal and culinary use. *"The Priory garden was well stocked with all kinds of vegetables, savoury and otherwise, to give zest to fasting days, and with herbs famous for their medicinal and healing qualities. The plant vulgarly called 'monk's spinage' is still found growing wild in the neighbourhood, and is perhaps a lingering remnant of what the Priory garden contained."* (The Antiquities of 'Moche' Malvern, by James Nott, 1885)

BENEDICTINE MONK.

Streams were channelled to create a large pond to breed fish for the monastery table, now *"Swan Pool"* in Priory Park, as eating meat *"flesh"* was banned by the Church. Although this provided some fresh fish, salted sea fish were also regularly brought from Bristol, but this was still not enough for the monks' needs and so abstinence from eating meat was eventually waived. *"Many inland monasteries were unable to obtain fish in sufficient abundance for their necessities. ... Vast loads of provisions were generally salted for supplies during the winter."* (Monastery and Cathedral of Worcester, by John Noake, 1866)

The bones of many animals dating from the 13th and early 14th centuries, farmed nearby or caught in the Forest, were excavated from a ditch at the back of Warwick House in 2004. Evidently the monks and their guests had eaten a rich and varied diet including beef, lamb, pork, goose,

chicken, wild rabbit and fallow deer. One bishop who visited the nearby manor of Colwall in 1290 *"with forty attendants, ate their way through a massive Easter feast of pork, poultry, 88 pigeons and no less than 4,000 eggs!"* (A History of Malvern, by Brian Smith, 1964) Eggs were another alternative to meat and a huge number of eggshells were also uncovered in Malvern. The lowest deposits also contained numerous fish bones including fresh water eel, pike, chubb, gudgeon and sea herring. *"A concentration of such waste is rare and is most often associated with large, well organised estates or large urban centres, usually of medieval or post-medieval date. ... Fishponds were expensive to maintain and were therefore only associated with wealthy or well-organised institutions."* (Report by the Archaeology Service of Worcestershire County Council, 2004)

As well as those living in and near the monastery, the ancient parish of Malvern included the inhabitants of the scattered local hamlets of Baldenhall, Guarlford, Poolbrook, Clevelode, Woodsfield, Newland and the Link. By the 13th century there were enough people living in and around the hamlet of *"Moche"* or Much Malvern for them to afford to build the separate little parish church of St Thomas near the Priory. It was finished by 1269 and survived for over three hundred years on the site of the present Post Office. The parish church was less than ten metres wide and thirty metres long, with a small chapel on the southern side, but this was enough space to house the fairly small congregation. In 1276 about a hundred heads of households in the parish were recorded as paying taxes to the Crown, so the total population could be estimated at fewer than four hundred persons.

By the end of the 13th century the Malvern Priory had become the main landowner in the parish, clearing and cultivating over a thousand acres to feed the increasing population. The main barn and farmhouse of the Priory, later called *"Nether Court"*, stood on the site of the present Council House on Church Street and a smaller farmhouse was inside the precinct gateway, supplied by the waters of the ancient St Agnes Well. Much Malvern's prolific water supplies were essential not only for the domestic use of the residents, but also for these new agricultural developments, including watering the farm animals, irrigating the crops

Great Malvern Priory and lands, with gateway to Southfield and Abbey Road c1810

and grinding grain into flour for bread at three watermills, driven by local streams. One mill was at Poole Brook, one in the Link and the other in Mill Lane, now Clarence Road, which was still in use in Victorian times but was demolished in 1903 after the natural water supplies diminished.

But in the autumn of 1314 heavy rains began to fall and the usual warm weather began to change with temperatures dropping by two degrees, bringing harsher winters and reduced harvests. This resulted in *"the Great Famine"* from at least 1315 to 1317, across North-West Europe and Britain. Standards of living fell drastically, diets became very limited, and people experienced increasing health problems as hunger took hold. *"People were driven to live on carrion; many starved to death, many were killed by bands of hungry robbers who roamed about seeking food, mothers hid their children to prevent their being stolen and eaten."* (Worcestershire Medieval Tax Rolls, from Rev. F.J.Eld, 1897)

76

Despite the risk of incurring huge fines, if caught, the records show that with harvests failing, ninety four people were arrested and accused of illegal hunting in the Malvern Forest in 1324. A list held in the British Museum shows that, unusually, the Vicar of Malvern at the little parish Church of St Thomas was replaced four times in 1338, suggesting that all was not well and famine or disease was in the hamlet. The income of Much Malvern monastery had already diminished substantially when, for two years between 1348 and 1350, *"the Great Plague"* swept the whole country.

Pottery had been made in the area of the Malverns from at least 500 BC. As Hanley Castle had a good supply of water from the Poole Brook and was close to prolific sources of red clay, in King John's reign it attracted further residents here to make pottery. At first they only paid a *"woodpenny"* for the right to collect windfall wood from the Forest to fire their kilns, but by 1295 were also being charged the substantial sum of 6s 6d a year to dig out clay at Blackmore Park. At the end of the 13th century sixteen working potters were transporting their fragile, heavy wares from the quay on the river Severn at Hanley, by boat to Worcester, Tewkesbury, Gloucester and Bristol. For fifty years their numbers grew until there were twenty six potters here, but in 1349 the settlement of about two hundred persons was infected by the Bubonic Plague carried by rats and their fleas from the river trade, and this terrible *"Black Death"* killed all the resident potters. Their original village of *"Potters' Handley"* was then abandoned. But it seems that years later pottery did continue to be made nearby, as in recent times *"Eight thousand shards of pottery dating from the 15th to the early 17th century have been recovered from just two fields on the north side of Roberts End, including bowls, fish dishes and jugs."* (Hanley History Website, 2009)

But in 1337, on the very eve of the first wave of the Black Death, England and France began fighting against each other in what would become known as *"the Hundred Years' War"*. Already suffering from malnutrition, poverty, disease, hunger, and now war, the arrival of the Black Death had a devastating effect on the weakened population in Europe and Britain, reducing it by between a third and two thirds. This *"Great Pestilence"* was said to have been triggered by huge earthquakes in the continent of Asia during 1343, which threw up *"pestilential fogs"* that darkened the skies. The disease travelled rapidly through China, India and Persia, killing many millions of people, arriving in Italy and then France three years later. The Bubonic Plague inevitably spread into England through the southern coastal ports, killing at least one and a half million people out of an estimated population of four million.

The uncertainty of daily survival created a general mood of fear and deep depression, many people believing that only God's anger could produce such a horrific illness. As so many of those who contributed money to the Church were now dying, the Church's revenues and donations again diminished substantially. The situation was made even worse when Edward III and his noble landowners raised the level of taxes, rents and fines, in order to sustain their own relatively high standard of living, reducing the Church's income still further.

Effects of the Black Death from the Toggenburg Bible, 1411

By then diseased and infirm patients had been attracted to the Malverns for at least two hundred years, as remarkable cures had been attributed to its holy waters. *"From the most remote times, the maimed, the lame, the halt, the blind, the leper sought to lave in the health giving waters, and to be made whole." (May's Guide to Malvern, 1886)* But now throughout the country lepers, beggars, foreigners and those with skin diseases, were all suspected of carrying the plague and their persecution and murder soon became common. In many areas of Europe Jewish inhabitants were also driven out or exterminated, after being accused of causing the disease by poisoning the water in wells. Jewish names had already disappeared from parish records in Worcestershire, including Hanley Castle, as Edward I had expelled most Jews from England in 1290 for usury; the practice of charging interest on loans, which was forbidden to Christians.

It is said that as early as the 12th century the Benedictine monks at Little Malvern used to wrap the diseased parts of sick patients in wet cloths at Holy Well. The Rule of St Benedict states that *"before and above all things, care must be taken of the sick, that they be served in very truth as Christ is served".* But now across England many caring monks became infected by their patients and died of the plague. The huge numbers of deaths depopulated the monasteries and universities and brought further rapid changes of incumbent parish priests, as well as a scarcity of labourers to bury the dead in the overflowing graveyards.

Monks, disfigured by the plague being blessed by a Bishop - Omne Bonum by James le Palmer, 1360-1375, the British Library

In the county of Worcester, *"in 67 parishes out of 138, the incumbents changed at this time ... At Great Malvern new priests were presented on the 10th July and 21st August. In the city of Worcester, as early as April, difficulties as to the disposal of bodies were forseen and provided against by the Bishop, Wulstan de Bransford, who himself, an old and infirm man, died on the 6th August 1349."* *(The Black Death, by Francis Aidan Gasquet, 2004)*

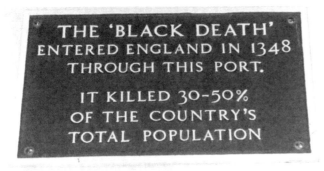

Much of Herefordshire and Worcestershire, including Malvern, Colwall, Hanley and the City of Worcester were devastated by the *"Great Pestilence"* in 1349 and most were infected again in 1361. By 1350 the plague had diminished the number of monks at Much Malvern to only ten and the parish had been reduced to absolute poverty. As so many of the peasant labourers had also perished, a third of the land in the county was no longer cultivated. By the end of 1362 the main outbreaks of the Black Death across the country had subsided, but over the following years there were further outbreaks in 1369, 1379 to 1383, 1389 to 1393, and throughout the first half of the 15th century. The Bubonic Plague returned to London again in 1603 and killed an estimated further 30,000 people, twenty percent of the city's population, spreading intermittently into England between 1636 to 1665, killing 45,000 more.

A sick patient being nursed in bed, Malvern Priory miserecord, c1350

Throughout the three centuries of the plague, tombs carved with morbid *"memento-mori"* became increasingly popular, reminding congregations of their mortality and the transitory nature of worldly things, the triumph of death and decay. One extraordinary example exists in Tewksbury Abbey; a grisly portrayal of a skeletal corpse, known as *"the starved monk"*, being devoured by a worm, rat, frog and a snail, but the person it commemorates is unknown. Legend claims the monk was found covered

80

Mid 15th century "memento-mori" sculpture in Tewksbury Abbey, Gloucestershire

in these animals, having died from starvation when stuck inside a hollow tree, where he had hidden during the Dissolution of the monastery in 1540. But the style of this monument has been dated to the famine and plague period at least ninety years before the Dissolution. The sculpture is also inaccurately known as the *"Wakeman Cenotaph"* in memory of the last Abbot of Tewksbury, John Wakeman. But the Abbot was made the first Bishop of Gloucester in 1541, dying in 1549 and he was buried in Forthampton church, apparently long after the monument was carved.

In Malvern Link a roughly cube-shaped stone, now beside the path through St Matthias Churchyard, may have had some links to the plague years. It is known as the *"Hoar"* stone, actually meaning 'ancient' stone, and was already considered to be a very old stone when it was noted as a boundary marker in Elizabethan times. As it has several rows and groups of small 'cup-marks' on its sides, similar to those found on some ancient Celtic stones, it may be very old indeed. The stone also has a hollow receptacle carved in the top where it's said *"Wroth Silver"*, a Saxon toll payment for safely crossing a boundary, used to be left and where coins are often still left today. There is an old local story, that plague victims used to leave money on the stone as a votive offering in the hope of a cure, or in return for food to be left there.

According to a map of 1633, this stone, recorded then as the *"Whore Stone"*, used to be in the centre of the crossroads above the Link common, near the site of today's Trinity Church. Many superstitions were associated with crossroads in medieval times. It was often believed to be unlucky to pass over such road junctions without stopping to leave an offering in respect for the sacred cross made by the tracks. In Worcestershire, magical cures for warts might be gained by secretly leaving a hazel stick by moonlight on the crossway, with as many notches cut in it as warts, but the affliction was said to be inherited by anyone who picked it up. People did not linger at crossroads during the night as lost souls or ghosts were believed to be held there, confused by the choice between the four different routes. For this reason gallows were often erected there, to hold the unquiet souls of the hanged and of suicides, who were often buried near these spots. To protect the soul of a dead body being carried to a cemetery, *"Corpse ways"*, paths along which coffins were taken, usually tried to avoid such crossings.

The 'Hoar Stone' now in Malvern Link graveyard

Perhaps to supersede such superstitious beliefs, these crossroads were often the site for a Christian stone cross and some claim the Hoar Stone became the base of one. In Malvern until about 1850, funeral processions crossing to graveyards at Leigh or Bransford always stopped here, to ceremonially rest the coffin upon the stone. Brief prayers were usually then said for the departed soul, the bearers exchanging positions on the corners of the bier before the corpse was taken on to the cemetery for burial. After the consecration of St Matthias Church in the middle of the Link in 1846, the stone was moved into their graveyard beyond the end of Hamden Road, where it remains; suggesting that its ancient association with the souls of the dead was still remembered and respected.

The sundial from the top of the preaching cross in Great Malvern Priory graveyard

Chapter VII

From Regeneration to Dissolution

Before the famine and Black Death arrived in the 14th century, life in the parish of Malvern had been flourishing. Despite the sudden change in climate, the failed harvests and famine, followed by at least twelve years of known Bubonic Plague in the area, the little village at Much Malvern managed to survive. But although the plague had faded, epidemics of other severe contagious diseases followed at intervals of about thirty years, until the end of the 17th century. These other 'plagues' also killed many and wiped out entire families in Upton, Hanley, Castlemorton and Much Malvern, causing a decline in the population of the area. Although this prolonged threat and fear of disease and death had severely demoralised the country's inhabitants, the gloomy mood gradually began to lift after Henry V and the English long-bowmen defeated the French at the battle of Agincourt in 1415. The King also deliberately wrote his campaign reports in English, symbolically ending the status of French as the official language in England. A new era of national pride and prosperity was beginning.

During the following period of regeneration, life was still very harsh and due to contaminated water supplies and insanitary living conditions, many people suffered from persistent infections of the eyes, skin and stomach. But such illnesses often responded well to drinking and bathing in the pure hill waters of the Malverns. In the 18th century Dr Nash recorded that the spring at the Holy Well had been *"long used with great success, particularly in disorders of the eyes, scrophulos cases, old ulcers, leprosies and other diseases of the skin"*.

This regular flow of sickly visitors still often sought the monks' help and the monastery continued to care for them, as well as feeding the local poor and hosting noble guests. Having survived the famine and the main Bubonic Plague years, in the early 1400s the Malvern monastery and its finances had recovered sufficiently for them to build a substantial timber guest-house or *"Guestenhall"* for visitors, just inside the gateway to the precinct, which survived until 1841. Almshouses where the sick could be hospitalised were also built on the *"Spytylway"*, a track-way that is now Church Street. In the Medieval period the term 'hospital' encompassed hostels for travelers, homes for the blind, the lame, elderly and mentally ill, plus dispensaries for poor relief, as well as clinics and surgeries for the sick and injured. During the 15th century the Malvern Priory was maintaining *"twenty-six monks and thirty poor men, in addition to discharging the duties of hospitality"*. *(Great Malvern Priory Church, Rev. Canon Anthony Deane, 1914)* Monastic hospitals developed many treatments, both medicinal and spiritual, and patients were encouraged to help each other through calmness and prayer, perhaps benefiting as much from this as from any physical treatment available.

The 15th century guest-house or Guestenhall, later used as a barn, by J. Basire 1837

Local residents now included a growing community of craftspeople living in small half-timbered, thatched cottages nearby. As well as the original tanners, bakers, charcoal burners and brick-makers in the parish, their skills now extended to glovers and shoemakers working with leather. John Noake recorded that *"Hides were furnished for harness, boots and shoes; and tallow for candles, which were frequently made in the monastery"*. With increases in sheep farming, others learnt to be spinners and weavers of sheep's wool, and by 1468 the first musician was mentioned, one Robert Haynes, *"mynstrell"* of Little Malvern.

After the outbreaks of Black Death had ended *"Benefactions to the Church were no-longer contributed entirely or at least chiefly, by the great nobles, but were now the gifts of the burgher folk and middle classes". (The Black Death by Francis Aidan Gasquet, 2004)* With these donations the monks could begin renovating and extending the old Norman Priory building, under the guidance of the youthful Sir Reginald Bray, master-mason, with King Henry VII donating the new *"Magnificat"* north window. Medieval potters now also began to work here, probably lay craftspeople rather than monks. They produced many distinctive red and white clay tiles with a transparent yellow glaze, some dated 1453 and 1456 on their edges, from a large double kiln which was excavated near the Malvern Priory in 1833, which still contained a few tiles. *"This kiln was about seven feet under ground, and consisted of parallel arches about thirty-five feet long, two feet three inches wide and*

The pottery kiln excavated beyond the eastern end of the Priory in 1833

fifteen inches high. Below the floor was the fireplace, about fifteen inches in height. This kiln was situated about two hundred yards from the east end of the church." (The Ancient Malvern Priory, Stevens, 1914)

When the Priory building was reconstructed from 1440 to 1500, over a thousand of these new decorative tiles were originally used to cover the curved wall behind the high altar and the floor of the church. Before the surviving floor tiles were moved to their present wall positions in the 19th century, the famous architect Pugin remarked that *"The pavings are decidedly the finest in the kingdom; such a variety of patterns and such a quantity of tiles I never saw anywhere"*. Some similar tiles, which still exist in the medieval churches of Worcester, Hereford, Gloucester, St David's and Monmouth, are now thought to have been produced by the potters from the Malvern Priory.

There are over one hundred different designs on the tiles in Malvern, including the arms of great local families and benefactors, sacred symbols, religious texts, moral sayings and legends. Some seem to address issues raised during the plague years. On a pillar near the Priory entrance a single prominent tile extols worshippers not to put off giving donations to the church until after their death, when the money will be in the hands of their executors. Another, sometimes known as *"St Agatha's Tile"*, bears an inscription from *"a book of charms"* compiled by a monk in the mid 15th century to heal various illnesses, and is now in the British Museum. The text refers to 'fire' or 'fever', a plague symptom, and this little Latin quote seeks to focus the mind and calm a feverish disposition, simply translating as, *"A holy mind, honour freely rendered to God, and liberty to the country"*.

The famous *"Leper's Tile"*, actually a square of four tiles, quotes a

significant biblical verse from the Book of Job often associated with burials, *"Have pity on me, have pity on me, O ye my friends for the hand of God has touched me"*. At the Priory it's believed that visiting lepers were now hidden from view inside the northwest entrance to the church, in a wooden shelter below the first window, which consequently has a higher sill to prevent other worshippers seeing them. *"In the middle ages there were many people smitten with such diseases as required isolation from their fellows and separate places were provided for them in the churches."* (Malvern Priory Church, James Nott, 1895)

Several early records from before 1537 note that Much Malvern's little parish church was originally dedicated to St Thomas of Canterbury, who had been martyred in 1170. On 29th December four royal knights had murdered Archbishop Thomas at the main altar within the sanctuary of Canterbury Cathedral. This violent action was in response to an appeal from King Henry II, who is said to have raised his head from his sickbed and shouted, *"Will no one rid me of this turbulent priest?"* But the people were so outraged that the King performed a demeaning penance, being flogged and walking barefoot to the cathedral. Becket's remains were placed in a golden shrine in the Trinity Chapel and for over three hundred years his entombed body apparently caused many miracles, becoming one of the most popular sites of pilgrimage. To avenge the humiliation of the King, in 1538 the shrine and Saint Thomas' bones were destroyed on the orders of King Henry VIII, who commanded that all mention of Becket's name be struck from the records to obliterate his memory.

Alabaster carving of the martyrdom of Archbishop Thomas Becket, 15th century, in the Victoria & Albert Museum

The original dedication of Malvern's parish church now seemed to be a liability and, probably in fear of the King's wrath, its name was quickly changed to *"St Thomas the Apostle"*. But despite this prompt action the congregation were evidently still reluctant to use the old church, and by the Dissolution of the Malvern Monastery it had fallen into total disrepair. In about 1540 *"the church of St. Thomas was taken down, its valuables were removed, and its font taken to St. Leonard's, Newland. On removing soil when making foundations for the music saloon* (19th century)*, a "piscine" of early date and portions of a floriated cross were dug up".* *(Some of the Antiquities of 'Moche' Malvern, by James Nott, 1885)*

To avoid both the controlling power of the Papacy and the excesses of the Protestant reformers in Europe, Henry had passed *"the Act of Supremacy"* in 1533, declaring that he was the head of the Church in England. Also in need of funds to replenish his royal coffers, he then ordered *"the Dissolution of the Monasteries"* across the country, during which many church treasures, revenues and possessions were confiscated by the Crown and their monastic buildings sold and dismantled. Unlike some other local monasteries, by then the Benedictine Priory at Much Malvern was not considered to be corrupt and even the supporter of the Dissolution, Bishop Latimer, pleaded unsuccessfully for it to be spared, saying that the Prior was "*an honest man and a good house-keeper; he feedeth many and that daily, for the country is poor and full of penury*". However, the Prior and monks were scattered from Malvern in 1539. James Nott wrote that after the closure of the monastery "*None mourned its fall more than the neighbouring poor*".

Malvern Priory and Gateway in 1787 by S. Hooper

The Malvern Priory precinct in the late 18th century

The Crown sold the monastery cloisters, farm, domestic buildings and Priory Church to William Pinnock, who sold them on a year later to John *"Knottesford"*, sergeant-at-arms, to undertake their demolition. He soon dismantled the domestic parts of the monastery including the cloisters, chapter-house and monks' dormitories, selling off the materials, probably mostly timber, and at that time all the monastery records were lost or destroyed. He also started to demolish the Priory Church, beginning with the Lady Chapel and south transept, selling the bells, the reusable stone and 74 tons of lead from the roof. As even the top of the preaching cross in the Priory grounds was regarded as an emblem of the Papacy, it was cut off and replaced with a sundial, symbolising the light brought by Henry's new Church. *"After the Reformation, crosses were often cut down halfway, or stumped, to put sundials on, telling that time was passing and much had to be done."* (Malvern Priory Church, James Nott, 1895) Having reputedly fallen from its high perch, Malvern's elaborate four-sided sundial, restored by the Friends of Malvern Priory in 1982, can still be found in the churchyard.

Elevated sundial beside the 'Pepper Pot' in Upton on Severn

The alabaster tomb of John Knotsford in Great Malvern Priory, c1590

To replace the derelict little church of St Thomas, in 1541 an enterprising resident named John Pope purchased the damaged Priory Church from Knotsford for the parish, saving it from total destruction by managing to raise £20 in two instalments from the villagers. Knotsford died in 1589 and is represented lying beside his wife on an elaborate Elizabethan tomb in the south-eastern corner of the church that he had once begun to destroy. His effigy is surrounded by the figures of four of his daughters, carved in relief on the sides, while his eldest daughter Anne, who commissioned the monument, is portrayed in a separate sculpture kneeling in front of his feet. The entire tomb, intricately carved from alabaster, originally with colour and gilded detail added, has survived relatively undamaged to the present day, on the right of the main altar.

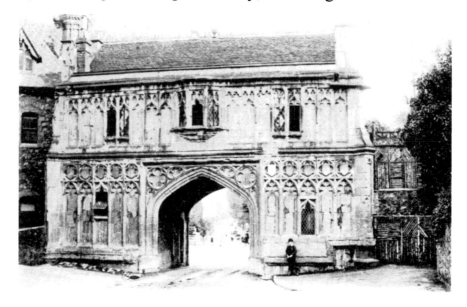

The Priory Gateway photographed before its 'restoration' in 1891

The original Priory Gateway also survives, but now with the elaborate castellations added during 'restoration' in the 19th century, and today it houses the local museum. The Holy Well itself was sufficiently valued for it to be given as a reward to John Hornyold in 1558 by Queen Elizabeth I and it was still in his family's ownership in 1919.

After five hundred years of Forest Law, during the reign of an impoverished Charles I, the Crown surrendered its rights and the Foresters' court ceased to exist. *"No more rent oats and rent hens the Lord be thankit, no more shutting up poaching prisoners in our Banbury Chamber at Hanley Castle, no more hanging." (Notes from The Feoffee Book at Tewksbury, Mr H.P. Moore, 1882)* The lands reverted to a Chase with only one third retained by the Crown, who then sold these off to Richard Heath and Sir Cornelius Vermuyden, a Dutch engineer involved in draining the marshes of the Chase. The rights and restrictions over the remaining areas were not clearly defined at first and uncertainties over their fair division and use led to local disputes and several riots. To discourage paupers from putting up hovels, for some time no new cottage was allowed to be built here unless it was on a plot of at least twenty acres. Both residents and those peasants who had 'squatted' within the Chase boundaries and so become self-appointed *"sole proprietors"*, were furious at these proposals. But when the remaining two thirds of the Chase were set aside by the King with rights of *"common pasture"* for those residing in local parishes, some of these grateful new 'commoners' then became staunch Royalists.

According to Nash, the Royal Forest was eventually completely *"disafforested"* on May 12th 1631, finally removing the legal designation of 'Forest' from these lands and bringing the great changes that gave us the landscape we are now familiar with. *"Here and there was a great turf glade and a forest pool surrounded by dells of greenery, but this was all now at an end, for down came the forest trees, and farms and*

Typical 17th century peasant's thatched cottage on the Chase

peasants' houses were erected on the haunts of the deer and wild boar. Great commons and long downs succeeded the dense bush, and the partridge and hare took the place of the stag and hind." (Hanley Castle by W.S. Symonds, Rector of Pendock, 1883) Even now many of Malvern's resident freeholders may still be entitled to 'commoners' rights' to graze sheep on the hills and commons and to collect windfall wood for fuel or fence repairs, although very few people exercise these rights today.

The twin peaks of the Ragged-Stone on the Malvern Hills

Chapter VIII

Tales of Corruption and Conspiracy

During the devastating years of the 14th century, attitudes had begun to harden towards the traditional feudal structures of both society and the church. The scarcity of manual workers now led some landowners to begin to recognise the value of the surviving peasants and their labour. The practice of *"boonworking"* for lords of the manor, where their villeins and serfs had to work without pay, had already begun to diminish by the time Madresfield Court changed to paying in cash for its peasant labour. When the neglected Norman churches were refurbished in the 15th century with expensive new displays of visual ornamentation, criticism of the wealth and corruption in the Roman Catholic Church also increased, and at the time it was claimed that the Church had *"shrivelled into a self-seeking priesthood"*.

One of the earliest mentions of the Malvern Hills by name was made in the long allegorical poem *"The Vision of Piers Plowman"*, a social satire, unusually written in the local Midlands Middle English dialect, rather than Latin. Its author was probably a secular priest called Robert or William Langland, writing in the mid 14th century. The poem creates a vivid picture of life in the Malvern countryside and

Medieval monk writing in the cloisters, 19th century

in a city, with a moral critique of the dishonest acts and corruption of the priests, their rich overlords and the impoverished peasant labourers.

Little is really known about the author of the poem and because of revisions in the texts of the three earliest written manuscripts, some have attributed the poem to other writers, including John Wycliffe and Geoffrey Chaucer. Some scholars claim that William is only the name of the fictional character in the poem, not that of the author. The poems' narrator, *"Will"*, has fallen asleep beside a babbling brook on the Malvern hillside. Here he dreams a vision of the landscape below as *"a fair field full of folk"* living between a tower on a hill and a dungeon in a deep valley, symbolising mankind between heaven and hell. The poem is considered by many to be one of the great works of early English literature along with Chaucer's Canterbury Tales and the story of Sir Gawain and the Green Knight, but there are no contemporary records of who the writer actually was.

"Then I began to dream a marvellous dream,
That I was in a wilderness, I knew not where.
As I looked to the east into the sun,
I saw a tower on a summit, worthily built,
A deep dale beneath, a dungeon therein,
With deep ditches, dark and dreadful to see.
A fair field full of folk I found between them,
Of all manner of men, the rich and the poor,
Working and wandering as the world asketh.
Some put them to plough, with little time for play,
At setting and sowing they sweated right hard
And won that which wasters in gluttony destroy."

Painting c 1940, by Alice Woodman of "A Fair Field Full of Folk ... All manner of Men", once in the Beacon Café and now in the Hills Conservators' offices

In the 18th century Nash said that the author may have been *"John Malvern, a Benedictine monk, of Worcester; who flourished in 1342"*.

Earlier records in the Bodlean Library show that one *"Johannes Malvernius Wigorniensis"* was a scholar and fellow of Oriel College, Oxford, and that his secular name was Robert Langland. *"Robert Langland is called by some John of Malvern, he is moreover reported to have excelled amongst the most elegant poets of his time". (History and Antiquities of the University of Oxford, by Anthony Wood, 1674)* It seems that both he and a John of Painswick became Priors at Malvern Monastery during the year 1349, but that Langland soon gave up the post to concentrate on writing his poem. *"Malvern's quiet cloister saw him slowly accomplishing his work, and by the year 1362 the poem went forth." (Antiquities of 'Moche' Malvern, by James Nott, 1885)* Local tradition claims he wrote the poem in the rooms above the Priory Gateway.

Medieval monk working in a monastic scriptorium, 15ᵗʰ century

Robert *"Langelande"* is also believed, by many, to have come from Colwall and to be a secular priest, born *"eight miles from Malvern at Clebrie"*, thought to mean Colwall or Ledbury, not Cleobury Mortimer. According to a 15ᵗʰ century manuscript, Robert was the illegitimate son of Stacy de Rokayle, probably adopting his surname *"Langelande"* from the *"Longlands"* between Colwall and Ledbury, possibly his birthplace and the home of his mother. He was ordained as a young acolyte in Bromyard and renamed *"William de Colwall"*. After his monastic education William moved *"moneyless"* to London in about 1355, where, as a chantry clerk, he was paid to chant funeral prayers for rich men. He married a woman called Kitte, had a daughter, Carlote, and lived in abject poverty at Cornhill. It was claimed that he spent most of his time continually composing and revising his poem, based on a quest for an exemplary Christian life, rather like *"Pilgrim's Progress"*, through life observed both in the crowded city and from the solitude of the Malvern Hills, the landscape and features remembered from his childhood.

Two hundred years later the first printed edition of the poem was published by Robert Crowley in the 1550s. It has been suggested that he wanted to reveal its relevance to the contemporary events of his time, seeking to show that the ordinary people were again suffering both economic and spiritual poverty, while some in the middle classes and aristocracy were using the Dissolution to gain more power and wealth.

Many men had acquired increased social status, as well as some wealth, by asset-stripping monastery buildings and estates across England. The destruction of both Great and Little Malvern monasteries was fairly typical. They were purchased, their buildings destroyed and the estates dispersed by John Knotsford, already a powerful figure in the area. Knotsford came from Hanley Castle and before the Dissolution had been a Ranger on the Chase, then Keeper of the Great Malvern Assart, and a Yeoman of the Guard. *"Unscrupulous and self-interested, he used these positions to his own profit, appropriating the Chase fees, reducing the numbers of deer drastically, and making an unprecedented income from dues rightfully received from the felling of forest timber."* (A History of Malvern, by Brian Smith, 1964) He used these monies to purchase the monasteries and, having demolished them, he moved into the Prior's house, beside St Thomas' Church in the centre of Great Malvern, living there for many years and becoming accepted into the Protestant landed gentry. On his death in 1589, the Priory estate passed to his daughter Anne, then to her husband's family, the Savages of Elmley Castle.

But across the country before the 16th century, reports of corrupt local clergy had also become common. Around the Malvern Hills the rector of Colwall was accused of fraud, while at Eastnor the rector was found to rarely appear in the church at all. The three priests at Cradley and Coddington were reported for neglecting their church services, perhaps because each had a separate mistress whose noisy activities kept one village awake at night. One of these priests also used his church as a calf-shed and the graveyard as a pigsty. As early as 1298 a young novice monk at *"Lesser Malvern"*, Simon Chamberlayne, was accused of breaking his vow of chastity and marrying his lover, before even being given permission to give up his novice's habit.

As well as the monastery at Great Malvern, Prior Aldwin is claimed to have also founded the Priory at Little Malvern in 1127, which was then organised by the hermits Edred and Jocelyn. Under the jurisdiction of

Worcester Priory, it was used partly as a house of correction for wayward monks from Worcester and consequently gained a bad reputation. In 1299 Bishop Giffard appointed John de Dumbleton, a learned writer but a quarrelsome priest, as the new Prior. Feeling cut off in this tranquil backwater, he apparently destroyed the peace of the brotherhood by complaining loudly and often that he missed the intellectual stimulation and fine library of Worcester. He resigned in 1301, but to the alarm of the monks it seemed he might be made to stay. They wrote to the Archbishop pleading that he should *"stay at our expense in some other house of the same Order"*, as *"his return, we well know, would disturb the quiet of our whole community"*. Eventually the monks agreed to pay Dumbleton five marks a year to stay far away and continue his studies at Oxford, although this sum was often paid with some reluctance.

Remains of Little Malvern Priory seen from the east in the late 18th century

In 1302, William Mills, the newly appointed Prior, was soon demoted for misconduct but stayed on for a further twenty years, during which discipline became even more lax. This caused Bishop Cobham to eventually issue a list of twenty injunctions in 1323, which itemised the lapses in monastic ideals at the Priory, although the bishop did add *"We have found much more that is worthy of commendation than that which demands correction"*. But suspected misconduct included selling church property without authorisation, mismanaging legacies, taking fish from the fishpond reserved for the recreation of the sick, halving the donations intended for the poor, while favouring particular locals by supporting their studies with this money, neglecting and inflicting penance on seriously ill but unpopular parishioners, and harshly punishing one young

98

monk without any evidence proving his offence. *"The Prior in his desire to punish some delinquent should not assert that he has accepted the fact of the man's delinquency from the whole convent."*

One Victorian, Charles F. Grindrod, was possibly inspired to base his historical novel *"The Shadow of the Ragged-Stone"* on this last example of the Prior's actions. But in his book Grindrod claims that he based his story on an ancient manuscript lent to him by a Mr Aldridge, supposedly a descendant of the story's heroine Rosamond. Grindrod tells of a 14th century monk called Bernard, condemned by his Prior to crawl daily up Ragged-Stone Hill in penance for committing three sins. Firstly he was accused of slaying Sir Eustace Devereux, a shameful Knight who had slandered his mother causing her death, then of having a love affair with the maiden Rosamond, after he rescued her from the evil clutches of Devereux's brother, and finally of murdering an elderly Knight, Sir Edmund Dunstan, who was accidentally killed in a violent struggle. Each day the young monk crawled uphill on all fours, his hands and knees torn by the rocky ground, but always accompanied by observers. One day he was watched with some sympathy by his Prior and Archbishop Thomas of Canterbury, who then both descended to Birtsmorton Court below.

Entrance to Birtsmorton Court, a 14th century moated grange, c1900

When Bernard had again almost reached the rocky summit, a dark shadow fell over him and the exhausted monk exclaimed, *"My curse be on thee, thou Heaven-blasting hill, and on those which lay this burden on me, and on all that be like as they are! May thy shadow and my shadow never cease to fall upon them, and upon this place that holdeth them"*.

As he spoke he pointed to the Priory below, then to the Convent where his pregnant lover had been incarcerated, and lastly towards the Court where the Prior and Becket had gone. With his last breath he called out *"Rosamond!"* and *"a strange column of dusky cloud seemed to be rising from the very ground where Bernard lay, and which almost appeared to resemble the form of the dead monk"*. The story ends by telling how the shadowy cloud fell across Birtsmorton Court, the prior dying within a year, whilst Becket was violently martyred not long after.

The monk, Bernard, cursing the landscape below the Ragged-Stone, by Austin Spare, from the cover of the novel by Charles Grindrod, 1889

It is still said that a curious small column of cloud does occasionally form between the two peaks and roll down the hillside, *"resembling a cowled monk"*, and this seems to have given rise to local legends of the shadowy curse. But some said these legends dated back to the time of the Druids. The Rector of Pendock imagined that *"On one occasion as Priests, Druids, and Bards were marching in long procession through the forest in the vale, for the summit of the Ragged Stone, where the night was to be passed in religious ceremonies previous to the holocaust at the Mistletoe Oak, the dark pillar of the Ragged Stone overshadowed them and not one ever reached the hill alive."* (Malvern Chase, by W.S. Symonds, 1881)

One old superstition concerned all the families who had resided below at Birtsmorton, originally Brutes-morton, beginning with the Brute family in Celtic times, followed by the Ruyhalls and the Hakluyts. Locals believed that they had all died out completely as a result of living in the accursed shadow of the hill. The most popular legend is from the middle ages, when the Court at Birtstmorton was occupied by Richard Nanfan, a Cornishman, who had enclosed some common land used by the Priory. It was claimed that an angry monk then made a curse that whenever the shadow fell upon the Court their eldest sons would be dead within twelve months and any visitors would later die horrible deaths. Apparently, over the years several eldest sons of the Nanfan family did die soon after the cloud appeared, and visitors who were staying there died unpleasantly, including the martyr Thomas Becket and Sir Thomas Wolsey.

In 1502 Thomas Wolsey had been taken into the household of Sir Richard  Nanfan and was trusted to be the executor of Richard's estate. But one day while in the orchard reading, he fell asleep and the superstitious young Thomas woke to suddenly realise that he was under the cursed shadow. After Richard Nanfan's death in 1507, Wolsey entered the service of Henry VII, later rising into a position of great power as a statesman and then as Cardinal. When he tried but failed to obtain an annulment for Henry VIII's marriage to Anne Boleyn, he was arrested for treason. Torn between his loyalty to the Crown or to the Church, in great distress he fell ill and *"died broken-hearted"* in 1530. Later Malvern historians attributed his unhappy death to the Ragged-Stone curse.

They also claimed that the 19th century statesman, William Huskisson, who was born at Birtsmorton Court, had become the most recent casualty of the curse, when he became the victim of a railway engine in 1830, crushed to death under Stevenson's famous *"Rocket"*. *"The accursed shadow of the Ragged-Stone Hill fell upon him, and he was killed at the opening of the Manchester and Liverpool Railway."* (Notes and Queries for Worcestershire, John Noake, 1856) It is still said to be very bad luck to be caught in the shadowy cloud from the twin peaks of Ragged-Stone Hill.

After Cobham's criticism in the 14th century, the Little Malvern Priory was thought to have been reformed, but a hundred and fifty years later another visitor, Bishop Alcock, a statesman and architect, found that the religious duties and services were again being neglected and the buildings had fallen into a terrible state of disrepair. He banished the Prior, John Wyttesham, to Battle Abbey and sent the only four remaining monks to Gloucester Abbey for correction. Two years later, in 1482, the bishop sent them a letter saying that Little Malvern *"is notoriously known throughout all my diocese by the misliving and dissolute governance of the brethren that have been living in the place. ... The rules of that holy religion have not been observed nor kept but rather the said brethren in all their demeanor have been vagabonds and lived like laymen. ... I have built your church and the place of your living is sufficiently repaired"*.

Only then did he allow the monks to return, but now with strict instructions governing their behaviour, including that they were not to *"go into the town or the fields without an urgent cause, license asked, and obtained of the prior; and that he that is so licensed shall have a fellow with him"*. The reputation of the poverty stricken monastery never really recovered and shortly before its closure and dissolution in 1534, the Prior and the six resident monks were accused of regularly poaching deer from the Forest, whilst disguised in hats, cloaks and swords, and then selling the skins to a local tanner.

The ruins of Little Malvern Monastery

After the suppression of the monasteries under Henry VIII, his pious son Edward VI continued with the establishment of the English Protestant Church, but he excluded both his siblings, Elizabeth and Mary from the succession to the crown. However, not long after his death in 1553, aged only 15, Mary rode triumphantly into London with Elizabeth at her side. But Mary was determined to crush the Protestant faith in which Elizabeth had been educated. Once she became Queen she imprisoned Elizabeth for nearly a year on suspicion of supporting Protestant rebels. Discontent spread rapidly through the country, and many Protestants looked to Elizabeth as a focus for their opposition to Mary's religious policies.

Elizabeth was recalled to the royal court in 1555 to support her half-sister through an apparent pregnancy, but Mary was probably suffering from a painful cancer and died three years later, having recognised Elizabeth as heir to the throne. One of Elizabeth's first moves as Queen was to support the establishment of an English Protestant Church, of which she became the head, and this evolved into today's Church of England. In the following years of the Reformation many neighbours and families were divided by differences in both their religious and royal affiliations, revealed in conspiracies, plots and betrayals. As a direct consequence of these divisions, in 1586 whilst imprisoned in the Tower of London, one Roman Catholic, Thomas Habington or Habingdon, began researching Worcestershire's past from ancient documents held in Westminster.

Some say he was a Malvern man as the Parish Records show *"Elizabeth the wife of Thomas Abingdon of Malvern, was buried the 27 day Sep 1589"*. But the Thomas who became involved in the Babington Plot, a conspiracy to murder Queen Elizabeth I and place her rival Mary Queen of Scots on the throne, was born in Surrey and married to Mary Morley. Perhaps because he was the Queen's godson, he twice survived possible execution for his involvement in

THOMAS HABINGDON Esq.
Confined to WORCESTERSHIRE on account of the
GUNPOWDER TREASON PLOT.

Catholic plots, firstly against her and then against Parliament. Twelve of the Babington conspirators, including his own brother Edward, were executed in 1586, but Thomas was only committed to the Tower of London for his association with them. He spent the next six years imprisoned there, studying the earliest surviving antique documents and recording their historical connections with Worcestershire. On his release he was allowed to return to Hindlip House near Worcester, which he then converted into a hiding place for Catholic priests. He employed Nicholas Owen, a lay brother who was skilled in building priest holes, and for years secretly sheltered fugitive Roman Catholics and Jesuit Priests there.

The failure of the Gunpowder Plot to blow up Parliament in 1605 was thought to be due to their inadvertent betrayal by Thomas's wife Mary in a warning letter to her Protestant brother. Hindlip House was searched by Sir Henry Bromley, Thomas' neighbour at Holt Castle. Thomas was not present when the initial search began, but he returned while it was in progress and denied any knowledge of such men, offering to *"die at his own gate if any such were found in his house or in that shire"*. During a virtual siege of the house for two weeks, a total of eleven priest holes were eventually discovered. Hiding in them were the Jesuit priests and suspected plotters; Father Henry Garnett, and Edward Oldcorne who had lived secretly in the house for almost 14 years, plus John Wyntour, Stephen Littleton, Ashley, a lay brother, and Nicholas Owen.

Detail of a contemporary engraving of the 'Gunpowder Plot' conspirators, by Crispijn van de Passe the Elder, National Portrait Gallery

Although Habington claimed he had no part in the Gunpowder Plot, he was arrested for concealing traitors and condemned to death, but on the intercession of his father-in-law, Lord Morley, he was later released. However, five of the others were executed, while Owen died under torture in prison. Habington, now aged forty-six, was pardoned but sentenced to be confined to Worcestershire for the rest of his life. He spent his time here completing the first full historical survey of the county, including Malvern, compiled from the earliest surviving antiquarian records. He died at Hindlip House in 1647 aged eighty-seven, but left us a *"History of the Cathedral of Worcester"* and *"Researches into the Antiquities of Worcester"* in manuscript form.

In 1774 Dr Treadway Nash was given Habington's manuscripts to revise and publish, and he based his *"History of Worcestershire"* on these earlier works, to which all subsequent historical accounts of Malvern and the county are indebted. Nash wrote that *"Many alterations were to be made, and much was to be added to the materials already collected, as well as to supply defects, to bring the work down to the present time"*. Habington's manuscripts survived and were eventually printed by the Worcestershire Historical Society in 1899. As many of Habington's original sources have since been lost, his early research documents have proved increasingly valuable to scholars and historians.

'Witches'; a flying spell imagined by Hans Baldung Grien, German woodcut, 1508

Chapter IX

Worcestershire Witches and Telsters

Pear of the dangers of 'witchcraft' had become common in England and Europe in the 14th century, during the early years of the Renaissance, although such accusations were often used to threaten women, and sometimes men, in disputes over other matters. But part of the Church's canon law was an earlier 9th century text, the *"Canon Episcopi"*, which declared that there was no such thing as an actual witch and consequently that a belief in *"night-flying witches"* was heresy.

Throughout the Middle Ages there had been several strands in the practice of folk medicine, including belief in the power of charms, spells, astrology and mysticism, as well as prayer and herbal remedies. There were probably as many women as men practicing this early form of healing. The use of herbs drew upon the medieval Christian *"doctrine of signatures"* which stated that God had provided some form of cure for every ill, and that all natural things carried a sign upon them that gave an indication of their usefulness. For example the white spotted leaves of Lungwort bear a similarity to the lungs, so were used to treat a patient with lung disease. The success of herbal remedies was ascribed to their

action upon the four humours within the body, black bile, yellow bile, phlegm, and blood, each produced by a particular organ. The astrological signs of the zodiac were also thought to be associated with the organs and humours, which had to be in balance for a person to remain healthy. As well as herbs and astrology, blood-letting was often used to restore this balance.

A female physician blood-letting a patient, placing heated vessels over the cuts to draw blood. 15th century manuscript, British Library

Most monasteries had created herb gardens for use in the development and production of herbal cures, administered to the sick by monks and nuns. The Catholic Church taught that illness was God's punishment for sin and as penance the sick often went on pilgrimages to visit holy sites, particularly the tombs or relics of saints, praying for a miracle cure when all else had failed. It seems the Priory was often visited by pilgrims because it also held holy relics, including the heart of St Blaise, the patron saint of wild animals and of those with throat maladies. After the Dissolution Bishop Hugh Latimer preached to his Protestant clergy, "*I think ye have heard of St. Blesis's heart* (St Blaise) *which is at Malvern, and of St. Algar's bones, how long thay deluded the people; I am afraid, to the loss of many souls. ... to lie still asleep in all kind of superstition*".

In the later medieval period the all-male university faculties of medicine had developed, excluding women from the healing profession. By the 14th century the study of rediscovered Greek and Roman medicinal texts and of early 'science' at universities resulted in the first qualified Physicians and Doctors of Medicine. After this the persecution of village healers increased, often women with some knowledge of healing herbs, charms and potions, handed down to them through generations of ancestors. Society began to believe in the previous heresy of actual witches, fearing that traditional healers were working destructively, by using sinister supernatural forces. The Church now regarded witchcraft as a reality rather than a heretical illusion, and these ancient folk traditions as sorcery, punishable by drowning, hanging, or burning at the stake to purge their souls of evil. The new phenomenon of the diabolical witch was created and from the reign of James I the accused were prosecuted in court under the *"Witch Act"*.

Burning a witch in 1533

As well as a fervent belief in God and the Devil, a belief in the existence of witchcraft played a huge part in the practices of Elizabethan and Stuart England, affecting all classes and everyone from monarch, to priest and peasant. It was now thought to be an organised conspiracy with the devil, a dark reality whose practitioners posed an ever-present threat to the structure of the church and state. Whether any of the accusations of witchcraft were true, or whether they were politically or socially motivated malicious acts, throughout the following centuries across Europe, witchcraft was universally feared as **menacing** black magic.

The wilderness of Malvern Forest and Chase was said to be peopled with witches until the end of the 18th century. *"There were reputed witches at Malvern in the last generation; and at Colwall the common people are said even now to dislike pewits* (lapwings) *which visit the place, believing that their cry is 'bewitch'd, bewitch'd;' and should any person capture one of these birds he is strongly recommended not to keep it for fear of misfortune or accident. Peewits are believed to be departed spirits who still haunt the earth in consequence of something that troubles them." (Notes and Queries for Worcestershire, by John Noake, 1856)* Some people in Mathon believed that witchcraft made their pigs waste away and they would then slaughter the animal, burning a piece of the meat to purge the carcass and prevent the spell from passing on to those who ate the rest.

Ever since the ancient Celts had broken their swords, spears, and cloak pins as offerings left in springs, similar superstitious acts had been widespread. At some places people still made good wishes by casting bent pins into wells, but to activate a curse a wax doll stuck with pins was sometimes dipped into the water and hidden nearby. Witches were often physically examined for a *"diabolical mark"* on their skin, believed to be evidence of their *"pact with the devil"*. It was said that this mark, probably a mole or birthmark, would not bleed if pricked with a pin and this was soon regarded as a reliable test for witchcraft.

In Herefordshire, old Nancy Carter was mistakenly thought to have bewitched a young man and so was stuck with pins, as here drawing a witch's blood was thought to remove her powers. Around the Malverns stories of herbal healers or witches abound, ranging from the play the *"White Witch of Welland"* to the factual accounts of accusations of witchcraft in the 17th century, recorded in the Worcestershire Sessions Rolls. Some people assume that the area known as the Wyche Cutting, where the road cuts through the Malvern ridge, has a connection with witches and the existence of a *"Pixie Path"* nearby, may strengthen this idea. Controversially, a wind-vane in the form of a witch on a broomstick has been fixed on top of the local bus shelter.

"The Witch of Eldersfield", Mary Bolingbroke, was said to have been a famous 15th century herbal healer *"celebrated for her wonderful cures"*, who lived hidden in the Malvern Forest near Castlemorton. But this witch is pure fiction and only appears in the historical novel *"Malvern Chase"* by William Symonds in 1881. The story claims that she gained much of her knowledge from her father, the actual astrologer Roger Bolingbroke, but unlike him, she avoided execution. On 25th July 1441, whilst tortured on a scaffold in front of St Paul's Cathedral, Bolingbroke

had admitted to his part in a plot to use sorcery to cause the death of Henry VI. He had been arrested with three others, who were all accused of meeting together in secret to perform necromancy and black magic, by slowly melting a wax image of the King. Betrayed by John Hume, a priest, the group were found guilty and Bolingbroke was hung, drawn and quartered at Tyburn on 18th November 1441. His three companions also died horribly. Thomas Southwell, the Canon of St Stephen's Walbrook, after torture, died in prison the night before being sentenced. Margery

Witch with broomstick, fire and 'familiar' animal/devil, Malvern Priory miserecord

'Examination of a witch' by Thompkins Matteson, 1853, Peabody Museum, Essex

Jourdemayne, *"the Witch of Eye, beside Westminster"*, was burned to death at Smithfield as a witch and heretic, and Eleanor Cobham, Duchess of Gloucester, having performed a demeaning public penance through the streets of London, at first was locked away in the cathedral crypt on the Isle of Man, then imprisoned elsewhere until she died fourteen years later.

The accused in Worcestershire were often tried at the London Assizes, but few trial records of the outcome of these cases have been traced, although the Worcestershire Sessions rolls from 1660 to 1697 do record the complaints against many individuals, who were to be brought to court. The wife of Edward Buckland was a midwife and was angrily charged by John Genifer, who owed them money, *"with being a witch, and deserved burning seven years since, and if she was a midwife was not fit to bring a ------- to bed, much less a woman"*. Although actual medicinal healing by women was outlawed, after the fourteenth century some were allowed to continue to function as midwives, often learning from a more experienced midwife, or a father or husband who was a Physician. The only qualification needed was a statement from a local priest declaring that the woman was of good character.

Women who became nuns often continued to serve as nurses, and there were also still some secular nurses, caring only for the physical needs of patients. Elinor Burt was accused of using witchcraft to heal *"several persons afflicted with diseases and distempers in their bodies"* and she confessed that *"she had a gift from God, by prayers and laying her hands upon their heads or faces, oftentimes to recover and heal them of their diseases."* Widow Bellet was charged *"for the evil art that she useth ... to find out goods lost, and using the name of Peter and Paul therein in profane manner."* Mary Slater was accused of bewitching a heifer to do it harm, and Margaret Hill was charged with using witchcraft for over seven years, whenever her neighbours refused her requests. The many accusations against her included making a child very ill by pricking its finger, causing a woman to be lame, killing a cow by stopping it giving milk, and causing pigs to foam at the mouth, fall over and die.

Witch, drawn in a margin, 1451

But Thomas Barnes, *"a person of good repute"*, made an official complaint that he had been falsely accused of witchcraft by Joseph Orford

110

of Oldswinford, a *"nailer"* and *"a common disturber"*. In return he now charged Orford with making threats to have *"Barnes and his wife ducked for witches"*. Some accused women also tried to fight back. After Joan Bibb was *"tied and thrown into a pool, as a witch, to see whether she could swim"*, in 1660 she brought a legal action against two of those involved, Justice Townsend and William Shaw the local parson, who were made to pay her £20 in damages by local magistrates. However, such accusations were difficult to shake off completely and she was then *"bound over for good behaviour, being of evil fame, and suspected of witchcraft, but not as yet charged"*. *(Notes and Queries for Worcestershire, by John Noake, 1856)*

When *"swimming a witch"* at Worcester, the accused were taken along *"Cucken Street"* to the river Severn, while in Upton they were ducked in a filthy pond at the end of New Street. Those who drowned were proven

innocent, but those who survived were presumed to be witches and were either killed on the spot or *"reserved for burning at the assizes"*. In 1649 four women were ducked at Worcester and having floated, were tried by local magistrates and found guilty. Margaret Landis and Susan Cook confessed while Rebecca West and Rose Holybred continued to deny the charges, but all were executed. Accused of

'Swimming a witch' accused of breaking a cart wheel and frightening the pigs, 1613, Bodleian Library, Oxford

poisoning her husband of only three weeks, newly-wed Ursula Corbett was also burnt as a witch at Worcester on March 14th, 1661.

Those who believed they were the victims of witchcraft often consulted *"a Telster, a wise man or woman"* for advice on what action to take, or how to remove a spell. In the mid 19th century Noake tells of *"the recent existence of 'the wise man of Dudley' and many others of the same class, though not quite so celebrated, who are now living"*. The last trial for witchcraft in England was in 1712 against Jane Wenham, *"the Wise Woman of Wakerene"* in Hertfordshire, claimed to have a reputation for *"swearing, cursing, idleness, thievery, and whoredom"*. She was found guilty but then pardoned, dying in 1730. But in Scotland, having given birth to a deformed baby, Janet Horne was burnt in a tar barrel in 1722.

The Witch Act was eventually repealed in 1736, stopping all legal prosecutions for *"conjuration, sorcery and witchcraft"*, but suspicion, accusations and duckings continued. In 1783 Dr Nash recorded that *"a poor woman who happened to be very ugly, was almost drowned in the neighbourhood of Worcester, upon a supposition of witchcraft; and had not a Mr Lygon, a gentleman of singular humanity and influence, interfered on her behalf, she would certainly have been drowned, upon a presumption that a witch could not sink"*. This gentleman, with enough status and courage to risk intervening in the ducking of an accused witch, was William Lygon, a County Justice who resided at Madresfield Court near Malvern. He had studied at Oxford and at the time of the incident was the Member of Parliament for Worcestershire. In 1806 he was made Baron Beauchamp of Powyke, a title that had been borne by his ancestors in the 15th century. He was created both the first Earl Beauchamp and the first Viscount Elmley in 1815 and died the following year in London.

But even today in the Malverns, these fears of witchcraft apparently still lie just below the surface. A letter, published in the Malvern Gazette only four years ago, complained about the centuries' old folk tradition of leaving flowers, prayers, and holy symbols as offerings of thanks for the pure waters at the Holy Well in Malvern Wells. These were mainly left by women, both local Christians and foreign visitors of many faiths. The symbolic meaning of these objects was interpreted by the letter writer as evidence of sinister dark practices, intimating that there were black magic ceremonies at the public well. This supposition then spread, causing concern to the local clergy and the current owner of the building, which resulted in these tokens being regularly removed and destroyed, except for the annual official well dressing of the site each May.

Well Dressing, Holy Well, 2007

It seems that these present day fears and suspicions of witchcraft are more difficult to eradicate than were the lives of the accused in Worcestershire's past history. During four centuries in Britain and parts of Europe, it has been estimated that a minimum of sixty thousand people were drowned, burnt, hung, strangled, or beheaded after being accused of witchcraft. About eighty percent of those executed were women.

Walkers on the hills at St Anne's Well, detail of an etching by J. Bradley c1825

Chapter X

Doctors, Donkeys and the Princess

n the 5th June 1607, John Hall, a well-established local Physician in Stratford Upon Avon, married William Shakespeare's eldest daughter Susanna. John Hall was noted for his professional approach to patients, irrespective of their social status or religion, and was considered to be medically ahead of his time. Books of herbal and folk remedies had been produced since about 1400 and were still being used by professional Physicians. In the 17th century, Hall published his own detailed medical case-notes as *"Select observations on English bodies, or Cures both empirical and historical performed upon very eminent persons in desperate disease"*. Here he recorded two hundred of his cases, providing a snapshot of the treatments and cures in use by Doctors at that time. A century before the repeal of the Witch Act, these still included old English folk remedies, such as a cloth dipped in frogspawn during a frost to stop a nosebleed, or applying two warm dead pigeons to cure arthritis, while three could cause an overdose.

As well as a continuing use of local 'witchcraft' remedies, from at least as early as the 16th century, Physicians began sending their patients to Malvern for the curative powers of the 'holy' waters. Before 1600, Jervis Markham, a gentleman in ill health, was sent by his Doctors to try various medicinal springs and so he came to the Malverns, where his health improved after taking the waters at *"Malvern-hilles-well"*, interpreted to mean the Holy Well. Having *"derived considerable benefit from the water"*, he wrote a long poem, the *"New Metamorphosis of J.M."*, which provided a very early testament to the medicinal fame of the waters here.

"But at that tyme there was wondrous fame
Of Malverne-hilles-well, for that bare the name.
For medi'cynable virtues from them all
Twixt both the Malvernes it from a hill doth fall.
Here I staid longer, that I might thereby
Experience learne, and the waters' virtues try.
Cures of some it did, both many and great.
It drew greate concourse to that pleasant Seate."

(The New Metamorphosis of J.M., 1600, British Museum)

On the rediscovery of this poem in the 20th century a local newspaper reported, *"We are perhaps, too much accustomed to think of Malvern's reputation beginning in the 18th century, and it is interesting to find that it was a popular health resort as early as the time of Elizabeth. And I think we may be sure that the virtue of the water was not a discovery of the Elizabethan age. The very name Holy Well suggests that it was given in the Middle Ages."* (Berrow's Journal, January 1921)

A hundred years after the visit of Jervis Markham, in 1708 a baby boy named John Wall was born nearby in Powick. He was to have a profound effect on the health and future development of the villages of Malvern Wells, Great Malvern and the City of Worcester. John Wall studied at Worcester and Merton Colleges, Oxford, taking his Medical Degree of *"Bachelor of Physic"* at St. Thomas' Hospital in December 1736. Four years later he married Catherine Sandys, the cousin of Lord Sandys of

 Ombersley. Lord Sandys Spout, a public but now polluted water source, can still be found in Spring Lane, Malvern Link. It was built in 1835 by a later Lord Sandys, who is said to have drunk the waters here every day, from the original Sandys' Spring.

In 1746 Dr Wall took up a post as one of the first four physicians at the Worcester Infirmary, a charitable new hospital, only the seventh to be built in the country. Nash remarked that as a Physician *"his benevolence displayed itself in its utmost extent in his unremitting attention to the poor"*. Three quarters of Worcester's population were said to be his patients and he consulted as far as Stratford on Avon, Kidderminster and Ludlow, where his visits sometimes lasted for several days.

In 1747 Edward Popham from Tewkesbury built a bath at Holy Well. By the early 1750's the pioneering Dr Wall believed that he had discovered scientific proof, through distillation, of the purity and effectiveness of drinking and bathing in the waters of Malvern's springs and sent some of his sick patients here to seek a cure. At that time the often unpleasant taste of minerals in waters was believed to signify their power to heal, yet Dr Wall promoted the unusually clean taste and purity of Holy Well as its healing power. This resulted in the popular rhyme, *"The Malvern water says Dr John Wall, is famed for containing just nothing at all."*

As well as his work at the hospital, Dr Wall with the apothecary William Davis, had been searching for a method of producing white porcelain, previously only made in the Far East. From 1743 they conducted their scientific experiments at Davis' shop in Broad Street, Worcester. European potters had been fascinated by this pure white china for hundreds of years and were now beginning to discover the secrets of its production. Wall and Davis founded a factory on Severn Street, i n May 1751, with the support of twelve investment partners, who had pledged to keep the porcelain formula secret or pay a large £4000 fine. The popularity of tea drinking in the 1760s brought them prosperity, creating a huge demand for their blue and white tea-wares, which did not crack when filled with hot liquid. After 257 years of manufacturing porcelain on the same site the factory went bankrupt, finally closing down in October 2008.

Commemorative jug produced in 1976

Part of the Royal Porcelain Works in Worcester, after its closure in 2008

During their search for the chemical formula, Wall and Davis had used distillation to analyse the waters from several of Malvern's springs,

116

particularly the Holy Well and Eye Well in Malvern Wells, plus the Chalybeate (iron) Spring in Great Malvern. Dr Wall then wrote an account of these *"Experiments and Observations on the Malvern Waters"* and at first these were published *"without a name"* in 1754, but then again in 1757 and 1769 by popular demand. The book was re-issued in 1780 by his son, Dr Martin Wall, Professor of Clinical Medicine at Oxford, and eventually included seventy-nine case histories of miraculous water cures, many at Holy Well. In these observations *"Several cases were described to prove the efficacy of the waters. They speak of weary treks by the sick and the lame through the pretty hillside village to the steep slopes beyond. There, at the well-side, their faith was rewarded and their limbs refreshed. One lady was quite blind when she was led to the well, but she so far improved that she was able to see a flea jumping on her bed".* (*The History of Worcester Royal Infirmary, William H. McMenemey, 1947*)

The profits from Dr Wall's book were *"devoted to assisting the many needy sick who came for treatment".* (*F.C. Morgan, Public Librarian, Malvern c.1930*) He also raised subscriptions from the gentry to make the Malvern springs *"more commodious"*, *"putting them in order"* by building wooden huts containing baths beside several, where an individual patient could bathe their afflicted parts more discreetly. The first public subscription list of donations towards providing permanent accommodation near the Holy Well was opened in September 1754, resulting in the building of the large *"Wells House"* in 1756, later a boys' school, then derelict, but recently converted into luxury apartments.

These early developments attracted a higher class of invalid to Malvern, with many more wealthy people now coming here to take the waters. In 1763 the Duke of York visited the Holy Well, commenting on *"the remarkable efficacy of the waters"*, after which its popularity with the gentry was assured. In 1773 the first well house was built over the existing bath and spring water supply. Dr John Wall retired in 1774, dying two years later, and his china was named *"Royal Worcester Porcelain"* by King George III, during his visit to Worcester in 1788. On his death the Governors of the Infirmary wrote of Dr Wall that *"In all concerns of life, and particularly in his practice, he was distinguished by an uncommon sweetness and cheerfulness of disposition: which in union with his extensive knowledge, and penetrating discernment, attracted the affection and secured the confidence of those who required his professional assistance. ... To his zeal and diligence the City and County of Worcester are in no small degree indebted for the advantage of their Infirmary. He gave it constant and regular attendance during his whole life, under very trying circumstances of fatigue and indisposition."*

As well as visitors to the healing springs, the little village of Great Malvern was now attracting cultured tourists and new residents seeking life in idyllic rural landscapes, away from the noise and grime of industrialisation. The ruinous state of the now neglected Priory attracted those in quest of the 'picturesque', although other visitors were highly critical of those who had permitted *"the defilement and neglect"* of this

Interior of the derelict Malvern Priory in 1807, with ivy growing inside the window

ancient building. In 1788 one shocked visitor wrote to the *"Gentleman's Magazine"* describing its condition; *"On the north side of the church was a play ground for unrestrained youth, whose recreation consisted in throwing stones at the numerous windows, all full of the finest stained glass; and adjoining this playground was a kennel of hounds, whose hideous yells filled up at intervals the interior of the church ... Here I saw actually stuck up on the eastern wall a large pigeon-house, belonging to the person who presided over the sacred place wherein I then stood."*

James Nott described how the church became *"in too ruinous a state to be used with safety"*. *"Rain came into the church in many places. Its many-times whitewashed walls were green in some places, and black in others with damp. The place had a vault-like smell. The few people who attended its once-a-week services had to wrap themselves up and take other precautions against catching their deaths."* By 1816, despite

widespread appeals for the *"fashionable of Malvern"* to make *"Christian and charitable contributions"*, only £9.19 shillings had been raised towards repairs, but then a government grant of £1000 enabled some restoration to begin under the new and enthusiastic Vicar, Dr Henry Card.

Ruined Priory, drawn in 1807 by Mrs Lathbury

Although these repairs prevented the total disintegration of the structure, after his visit in 1833 the famous architect, Pugin, disparagingly commented, *"Two hodfuls of mortar were got to repair the church, and the remainder of the money expended in putting in a window of the aisle, and the arms of the subscribers in stained glass, with their names in full, a monument of their folly and arrogance. The very mullions in which the glass is placed, are rotten and falling. The church itself is in dreadful repair; fall it must, and all that is to be hoped is, that in its fall it may annihilate those whose duty it was to have restored it."* He concluded by describing them as *"such a set of lounging idlers, the fashionable of Malvern are only to be matched at Brighton or Cheltenham"*.

The following year, perhaps in response to the now numerous critics, Dr Card again attempted the restoration of the church, with extensive repairs to the exterior of the north side, the battements and pinnacles of the nave and porch, excavating over three foot of covering soil from the base of the walls to allow them to dry out. By 1841 the remainder of the church's exterior had been renovated, with the exception of the tower. Three years later the Reverend Card died, and Nott wrote, *"The truth is, the taste for restoration of churches was not then so advanced as now, and he did what he could. He had to please those associated with him, or nothing in the way of money came in. To say the least, he saved the noble church"*.

In 1816 the village consisted of "*about 50 houses, chiefly neat buildings, to which are attached gardens and plantations of fruit, trees, shrubs and evergreens*". Of these "*twenty two were lodging houses, Tradesmen's and houses of entertainment*" including the Crown, the Unicorn Inn, and the Belle Vue Hotel with its stables at the rear and a main carriage entrance, now an arcade. "*About the spots occupied by these Hotels, the owners of Jerusalem ponies ply for hire: here are also to be let, Donkey carts, where the patrons of the whip may drive these animals curricle or tandem.*" (*A General History of Malvern, John Chambers 1817*) The very first resident doctor, "*A Physician of great eminence*", Dr Bennet Garlike, had now moved into Melton House on the southern approach to the village, (see plan at page 49, house no 60) "*where he intends to continue, and exercise his profession*". (*A Description of Malvern, Mary Southall, 1825*)

Malvern village with the Priory, first hotels and Library, seen from Hay Pool, 1825

John Downs had built the Downs' Hotel in 1810, which he soon renamed the Foley Arms in honour of the Lord of the Manor. Edward Foley was "*a gentleman possessed of very considerable property in the village and neighbourhood, and whose liberality of disposition, has always been conspicuous*". By the 1820s

Last of Hay Pool at Salisbury House in Abbey Road, below Baptist Church, 2007

Great Malvern's popularity was even more assured following the creation of the Library, and then the Coburg Baths and Pump Room next

120

door, directly opposite the Unicorn Inn with its central donkey stand. It seems these developments were the idea of *"our highly respected Lord of the Manor, Edward Foley, Esq. whose beneficence is unbounded, and at whose expense the Baths were erected, ... and the professional taste of Mr Deykes of London, his architect, under whose superintendence, Malvern can now offer a new feature of attraction to its visitants"*. *(A Description of Malvern, Mary Southall, 1825)*

The Coburg Baths, the first bath-house in Great Malvern for taking the waters, now Whatley Recordon Solicitors, 12 Worcester Road

The new Library in Great Malvern village, with its classical bow end, c1820

The elegant Library building, with its bow-fronted corner, provided a social and cultural centre, holding assemblies, conferences, balls and weekly "*Routs*" or parties. It also contained other attractions to entertain middle and upper class visitors; a reading room with newspapers, a music room, a billiard room and *"the Bazaar"* selling souvenirs, including some early prints by Lamb of the donkey rides, as well as *"snuff, patent medicines, stationery and a few other articles likely to attract the fancy"*. With the help of her husband John, the organist at the Priory, the Library was run by Mary Southall, who also wrote *"A Description of Malvern, a guide to the drives, walks and excursions"*, published in 1825. Accommodation and board cost the princely sum of two guineas a week, while a labourer's wage was just three shillings and six pence.

From the mid 18th to the early 19th centuries this influx of the gentry, in search of 'romantic' landscapes and also to 'take the waters', had resulted in the first wave of development of Great Malvern, from a series of hillside dwellings into a small spa health resort providing entertainments, with carriage excursions and hillside donkey rides to visit the springs and see the 'picturesque' views. *"The salubrity of the air, the efficacy and purity of the waters, the charming romantic rides and walks upon the hills and in the vicinity of Malvern, must necessarily cause this to be pronounced one of the most interesting places of fashionable resort in the kingdom." (A Description of Malvern, Mary Southall, 1825)*

Princess Victoria riding Moses at Holly Mount Cottage, drawn in 1830

In 1830 the Duchess of Kent brought the young Princess Victoria *"to stay at Holly Mount Cottage for several months. Here the child rambled freely in the woods and on the hills, and rode often on the donkeys, especially her favourite Moses, who thereafter was called 'Royal Moses',*

*Princess Victoria riding Moses down Victoria Drive from St Ann's Well,
by J. Bradley, published in 1831*

The popular donkey-stand on Victoria Drive in 1858, by Cuthbert Bede,
courtesy C & R Bannister

*attended by the donkey-woman in a bonnet and red cloak. ... She
performed here what was probably her first public function by declaring
open a new path made near St Ann's Well, from Nob's Delight to the
Foley Walk."* (A Little City set on a Hill by C.F. Severn Burrow 1948) This, and

other royal excursions, made donkey riding extremely popular here, and from then on the road that zigzags to the well house and to the summit of the Beacon was named as Victoria Drive and the road to Holly Mount Cottage later became Queen's Drive. During her ten-week stay Victoria also visited the Bazaar in the new Library building, which then became the 'Royal' Library, now Barclay's Bank on the corner of Edith Walk.

By the 1840s Messrs Lea, Perrins and Burrows had established a thriving chemists shop at the top of Church Street in Great Malvern and Burrows then began supplying bottled Malvern water to the public from their *"mineral water factory"* at the Holy Well, which Schweppes took over in 1850, then Cuffs. In 1838 Lea and Perrins began to sell the first bottles of a new relish *"Worcestershire Sauce"*, which proved increasingly

Holy Well and mineral water factory c1870

popular. The bottle's paper wrapper stated that the sauce came *"from the recipe of a nobleman in the county"* said to be Baron Arthur Sandys of Ombersley Court. It probably came from the baron's mother, Lady Mary Sandys Hill, but it would have been a breach of social etiquette to identify an aristocratic lady on a commercially bottled sauce. The recipe for the original mixture of curry spices is believed to have been given to Lady Mary by the visiting niece of the Chief Justice of India. The chemists Lea and Perrins then tried to make it up as a dry powder for her, later mixing it with vinegar, but it proved unpalatable and the cask was abandoned in their Worcester cellar for several years. Legend has it that they then tasted it again and found it was now a delicious sauce, which was marketed to the public and became a huge commercial success.

By then the Burrows brothers had begun bottling water at a site in Great Malvern, today Robson Ward's Kitchens store, and at the request of Queen Victoria and under great security, they supplied the royal family with table water from a secret spring on the hills above the town, until the 1950s. Today Coca-Cola still supplies bottled Malvern water to the royal household, now from the old Schweppes bottling plant in Colwall.

Horse drawn traffic passing through the Priory Gateway in Victorian times

Chapter XI

Hydro-therapy, Dust and Drought

o exploit the town's existing springs and wells, from 1842 onwards the Doctors James Wilson and James Manby Gully brought the practice of hydro-therapy to Great Malvern from Priessnitz in Austria, opening the first commercial *"water cure"* establishments in Great Malvern. Throughout the following thirty years the population increased even more rapidly as many well-to-do new residents, visitors and patients

Dr James Wilson and his family in Malvern, c1860, *courtesy of Malvern Library*

were attracted to Great Malvern, now known as *"the Metropolis of the Water Cure"*. They hoped to improve their health by taking the waters under the strict guidance of the growing multitude of expensive private water cure doctors, whose portraits were often hung as advertisements in the shop windows and inns. Malvern was prospering and it was said that, *"You only have to put out a bucket and gold sovereigns rain into it"*.

In the 1840s a manual labourer still earned about sixpence a day, but one week of the water cure cost about five pounds, over thirty times a workingman's wage, although Dr Wilson did give concessions to poorer patients. Malvern was now the fashionable health resort of the intelligentsia, favoured by many renowned politicians, scholars, artists, poets and writers. *"Charles Dickens spent some time at Malvern early in the fifties. The place was then the sole resort of hydropathy in England. Dr Gully was in the zenith of his fame; and Wilson's large establishment, and almost every lodging house in Malvern, was full of water patients."* (Malvern Priory Church, James Nott, 1895)

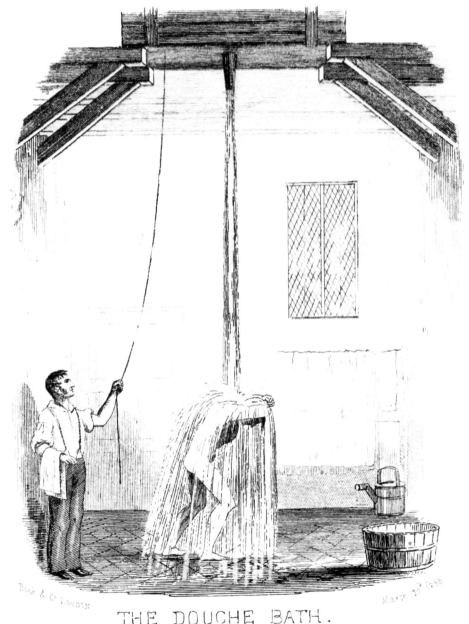

THE DOUCHE BATH.

In the 1850s the town's many famous visitors also included Wordsworth, Tennyson, Gladstone, Disraeli, Carlyle, Thomas Macaulay and Florence Nightingale, who came here ten times while convalescing after the Crimean War. Charles Darwin took the water cure when he was suffering from the severe gastric ailments he had had since his voyage on the Beagle. Already considered an atheist, he became even more disillusioned with the idea of God after his favourite, but sickly ten year old daughter, died at Montreal House in 1851, whilst also a patient of Dr Gully. Little Annie, *"a dear and good child"* is modestly buried under a tree in the Priory Churchyard. Knowing that it would

Annie Elizabeth Darwin

cause great controversy amongst Christians, it was not until eight years later that Darwin decided to publish his influential theory of evolution, *"On the Origin of Species by Means of Natural Selection, or the Preservation of Favoured Races in the Struggle for Life"*.

'Hydropathic Establishment' and baths built by Dr Wilson in 1847, now Park View

In 1851, for the first time, more people now lived in English cities than in the countryside, but Malvern continued to grow. The popularity of the little village brought rapid changes and in the same year it officially became a town. The very first railway branch-line from Worcester was constructed to Malvern Link in 1853 and the station was completed in

1859, delivering further water cure passengers in relative comfort, but they still needed equine road transport to complete their journeys. To help cope with all this extra traffic, from 1854 the streets of Great Malvern were watered every night and morning in dry weather to try to improve their worn and dusty surfaces.

Water cure visitors and donkeys at St Anne's Well, with the new octagon c1860

As the town's population increased, the prolific spring water supplies that had attracted so many people here began to prove inadequate. By 1855 the lack of rain, plus the now numerous hydropathic establishments taking supplies from the springs, caused increased shortages of water for domestic and commercial use throughout the Malverns.

By 1865 over a quarter of the new buildings were lodging houses using large quantities of water and John Noake wrote, *"During the last thirty or forty years Malvern has been rapidly growing as a place of resort, and is now become a town by Act of Parliament. A striking proof of its progress is afforded in the fact that in 1841 there were only sixty-four inhabited houses in the village, while in 1861 there were 992. ... The wet sheet and the douche bath are now in active requisition all the year round, there being located here no fewer than ten hydropathic physicians (independent of the regular faculty), and six establishments, devoted to this moist treatment."* *(Worcestershire Relics, John Noake, 1877)*

Malvernbury House & Dr Johnson's Baths, Malvern, 1862

The railway line connecting Great Malvern's new station to London was completed in 1861, bringing three thousand more visitors to the town in the first year, equalling the number of residents. In the same year, complaints from residents published in the Malvern Advertiser, reported that the town was being ruined by the drunkenness and bad manners of these day-trippers, so passengers on day excursions were made to alight at Malvern Link. By 1900 up to thirty-five trains a day were bringing regular floods of visitors here, including many day-trippers on excursions from Birmingham and the Black Country. This influx of ordinary tourists continued to cause much annoyance to Malvern's more genteel folk.

The hydropath, Dr Wilson, died in 1867 and the popularity of the water cure began to decline in the 1870s. His memorial, an elaborate fountain in Abbey Road, became badly neglected and was eventually demolished in 1945. Dr Gully retired and moved away in 1872, after an alleged love affair and being implicated in the scandalous apparent murder of Charles Bravo, the woman's husband. Dr Grindrod died in 1883 and the last remaining practicing hydropath, Dr Fergusson, was associated with an outbreak of Typhoid fever and went bankrupt in 1913.

The growing town of Great Malvern seen from North Hill, 1871

Great Malvern to Link Top seen from Pickersleigh, c1875

From the 1870s West Malvern became the centre for a circle of distinguished guests who stayed at the Westminster Arms and Ashfield House, including the poets A.C. Swinburne and Robert Bridges, Dr Jowett, Master of Balliol College, Sir Jesse Boot, herbalist and founder of

Boots the chemists, the theologians Dr William Temple, Archbishop of Canterbury and William Inge, Dean of St Paul's, and the Prime Ministers A.J. Balfour and Sir Henry Campbell-Bannerman. Dr Peter Mark Roget, physician and mathematician, better known for his *"Thesaurus of English Words and Phrases"* published in 1852, often stayed at the house. He died here in September 1869, aged 90, and is buried in St James' Churchyard. His life had been marked by several tragedies, including the early death of his father and later the suicide of his favourite uncle, the law reformer Sir Samuel Romilly, after the sudden death of his wife in 1818. Despite Roget's presence, four days later in shock and delirium, he managed to leap from his bed and cut his own throat. Roget's work on the thesaurus was part of his life-long battle with his own depression.

The lack of spring water in the Malverns continued to be a huge problem for many years, particularly following the "Great Drought" of 1887 when little rain fell. Then the British Camp Reservoir with a capacity of fifty million gallons was built to supply the town from the hill springs above. It was opened by the Duchess of Teck in 1895 amidst great celebrations and when filled by heavy rainfall the following year it was heralded as the solution to all Great Malvern's water shortages. But as demand again increased it soon proved insufficient, the reservoir drying up completely during the drought of 1902. The following year water began to be

permanently piped here from boreholes at Bromsberrow. The building costs of the reservoir, to be paid by the relatively small community of Great Malvern, reached the huge sum of £60,000 raised by loans for the scheme, which were still being paid back by the inhabitants in the 1950s.

Norman May's guide published in 1886 says, *"The Wells are less and less used for medicinal purposes, but are now kept in a condition to satisfy the most fastidious. In fact Malvern is no longer a place where the visitor is shocked and his feelings harrowed by troops of invalids; but is rapidly growing in favour with the robust, healthy and energetic, to whom its hills, golf links and splendid roads afford endless opportunities for recreation and exercise."*

132

Local children of poor families employed as hop-pickers, c1880

Chapter XII

Scholars, Soldiers and Social Change

Before 1830 the Right Hon. Apphia, Baroness Lyttelton, had sold the family silver to fund one of the first Sunday Schools in Malvern. *"When her ladyship married Colonel Peach, he presented her with a valuable set of filigree dressing plate. ... Finding the state of children about Malvern was miserable, from a total want of religious instruction, she resolved to honour the memory of the donor, by laudably applying the gift to the erection of a Sunday School."* (A Description of Malvern, Mary Southall, 1825) At first this school for the children of the poor was established above the Unicorn Inn, the public house still in existence today. In 1817 John Chambers wrote that Lady Lyttelton *"continues to watch over the morals of the lower orders of society round Malvern, in the welfare of which place she has always felt much interested."*

With the support of other local aristocratic benefactors, Lady Lyttelton soon followed this venture by founding a *"School of Ancient Industry"* to create her vision of a romantic rural idyll here. She encouraged women

---

SCHOOL OF ANCIENT INDUSTRY,

FOR SPINNING OF

Wool, Flax, Hemp, Knitting, &c. &c.

ERECTED ON MALVERN CHASE,

through the Liberality of

Lady Lyttelton,

Edward Foley, Esq., of Stoke Edith Park,

Earl Beauchamp, and others.

---

and children to return to work in the fields, rather than follow their new ambitions to become household servants for the increasing number of wealthier Malvern residents. *"Observing that at present, the peasantry of*

Great Malvern, are so earnestly desirous of obtaining light and genteel work, that the farmers find it difficult to procure weeders; and aware of the baneful effects arising from an improper love of dress among female servants, she has endeavoured to check the growing evil, and has suggested and supported, by her influence, this institution. ... In this manner they may learn to produce their own garments of a cheap and substantial kind, suitable for their condition in life, as in former ages. In

order to preserve to society, a useful hardy peasantry, it is intended to encourage field work; and that this employment may not be the means, as h e r e t o f o r e, o f corrupting the morals of young persons, one of the matrons of the school always attends and works with them."
(Description of Malvern, Mary Southall, 1825)

A typical family going to the fields at harvest time c1870

Much earlier, in the eighteenth century, there had been a small school on Belle Vue Terrace, where the annual venison feast was also held, but as the village began to attract more visitors it became the first hotel, the Crown, where Lloyds Bank now stands. The Crown was leased by both Dr Wilson and Dr Gully when they first arrived in 1842, renamed *"Graefenberg House"* and used to accommodate twelve water cure patients with *"indefinite diseases which a large income and unbounded leisure are so well calculated to produce"*.

As well as the Lyttelton schools, from the 1820s other smaller schools for either genteel boys or girls were held in numbers of the new boarding houses, but none of these survived for more than a few years. The benevolent Dr Grindrod, of water cure fame, helped the poor and illiterate donkey boys by founding a small school for them in the 1850s at the foot of the Worcestershire Beacon. Here they were taught the rudiments of 'the three R's', but it was closed down in 1870 when compulsory primary education came in. Another benefactor, Charles Morris, built the North Malvern National School for local children in 1838, on land leased from the Hornyold Estate. It survived until 1991, opposite his 'Tank' public drinking spout built for the poor in 1835, now known as the Clock Tower.

'Romantic' portrayal of farm-workers sowing seed, photo c1880

Impoverished women running a donkey-hire stand, Malvern Hills c1850 © *Bannisters*

136

The new Malvern College building in the 1870's

Ambitious proposals for a grand public school *"for educating the Sons of Gentlemen at moderate cost"* were discussed by the gentry in the 1850s. John Wheeley Lea, of Lea and Perrins sauce fame, offered £10,000 towards the cost of a new school building on the Lodge estate, owned by the Foleys. One of his partners in the Malvern chemists shop, Walter Burrow, became a great supporter of the scheme, but it seems that the gentry were unhappy with the prominence of 'tradesmen' in the plans and Lady Foley refused permission for the site to be on her land. Further

delays followed and the *"Malvern College"* was not built until 1865, eventually housing six hundred boys on twenty-six acres of land in South Field, owned by Dr Leopold Stummes.

By the time the boys' College opened there were at least sixteen other private schools in the Malverns and the numbers continued to grow until the end of the century. By the 1900s the name of the town was synonymous with the strict public school education of the children of the aristocratic elite, plus those from the wealthiest of the middle classes.

Chauffeurs waiting in Church Street

Towards the end of her life, Jenny Lind, opera singer and philanthropist, came to live at Wynd's Point, below British Camp, and sang at the opening of the Royal Malvern Spa near Wyche Cutting in 1883. She had become famous as the *"Swedish nightingale"* in the 1830s, performing in Europe and America. She died in Malvern from cancer on November 2nd 1887 and was buried in Great Malvern Cemetery to the music of Chopin's Funeral March. She left a considerable part of her wealth to help in the education of poor Protestant students in Sweden.

In 1868 a sickly William Ryland, the Mayor of Bewdley, had come to Great Malvern to take the healing waters to try to cure his tuberculosis, but without success. An old resident advised him as a last resort, to try the waters and air on the western side of the hills near the Wyche Cutting and after regularly drinking water here his health improved. The source was kept secret from him but he soon discovered the water was from St Thomas' Well, inside an old cottage, which he managed to buy. But local people resented Ryland's control over the well and burnt down the cottage. In order to placate them, in 1870 he built a public spout beside the highway, supplied from the original source, and from then on villagers Well Dressed it every year with a profusion of flowers and garlands. It had been named the Royal Malvern Well by permission of Queen Victoria, after her daughter Helena had visited and drunk its water.

With appeals to create a well room for the gentry, Ryland then went on to build an ambitious domed hall seating 2,000 people, *"opened in May 1883 by Jenny Lind, in the greatest grandeur,*

before a gathering of all the Worcestershire and Herefordshire elite."(*Worcestershire Archaeology and Local History Newsletter, 1979 No 26*) This included the main *"Spa Pump Room"*, a refreshment bar, a suite of water cure baths for *"tourists and invalids"* and an art gallery. The impressive Royal Malvern Spa building was likened to St Paul's Cathedral by the enthusiastic local press. In its first year Jenny Lind made her last public appearance in the hall, in aid of the Railway Servants' Benevolent Fund. But only two years later the attractive new Assembly Rooms in Great Malvern were opened and the Royal Spa became known as *"Ryland's Folly"*, closing down in 1895. Ryland was bankrupted and the site was soon vandalised and became derelict. It was demolished in 1937, but the original Royal Well public spout remains.

Oak tree paraded along Belle Vue Terrace at the marriage of the Prince of Wales in 1863, then planted on the common at Link Top

The turn of the century brought great changes to Britain and to Malvern. Unlike Queen Victoria, who died in 1901, her popular son King Edward VII, drank, smoked and loved high living, often visiting Great Witley Court for party weekends and becoming known as *"Edward the Caresser"* because of his many affairs. However, some anxiety began to be felt by the English aristocracy, following the first Russian Revolution in 1905. In Edwardian England the harsh divisions between the rich landed gentry and the poor led to unrest, with increasing demands from a growing working class for radical solutions to their poverty. At the same time the demand for more battleships, to match the worrying increases in the German navy, threatened the finances available for social reform, but proposed cuts in the number of ships then led to Union strikes by the dock workers. Dissatisfaction with the old social order was rife. Most working class men were disenfranchised, while men over twenty one who

owned land, or a house, or had a University Degree, were able to vote. Women had no vote at all as they were regarded as the inferior sex, destined for marriage and children, factory or farm work, home-keeping, or domestic service and they were the poorest, most exploited workers.

Suffragette Emily Davison falling fatally injured after her collision with the King's horse, 1913

Increasing numbers of protest actions by the Suffragette movement, led to the dramatic death of protester Emily Davison under King George V's racehorse in the 1913 Derby. Women in Britain eventually gained the vote at the end of the First World War in 1918.

In 1909 the Liberal Chancellor of the Exchequer, Lloyd George, introduced a revolutionary *"People's Budget"*, which aimed to calm matters by providing social insurance for the sick and infirm. But this was to be partly funded by the landed gentry through a sharp rise in tax on incomes above £3,000, higher death duties, and an innovative tax on profits from unearned increases in the value of land. In his famous Limehouse speech, Lloyd George lashed out against landlords, especially the aristocracy, who were becoming increasingly rich from rising

land values. Having angered the landed gentry, these proposals for social benefits were met with great hostility in the House of Lords where his budget was rejected. This led directly to the Parliament Act of 1911, in which the Lords lost their power of veto, severely curtailing the future powers of this upper house. Old-age pensions had already been introduced by Asquith as Chancellor and after the crisis of the *"People's Budget"*, Lloyd George also introduced National Insurance to provide workers with unemployment benefit. The nervous English aristocracy now began selling off many of their assets, to realise their value in advance of any new inheritance taxes. Huge sections of manorial lands in the Malverns came onto the market. In 1910 Lady Foley's grandson disposed of a large swathe of land and properties, from below the railway line in Malvern Link to Barnard's Green, as potential building plots to house Worcester and Birmingham commuters.

Gloucesters' camp on Wells Common, Berrows Journal

In 1915, a year after the outbreak of the First World War, Lloyd George came to Malvern and addressed the new 13th Gloucester Regiment stationed on Wells Common. *"One bystander asked him about the shell shortage at the front that had caused much consternation. The Welsh minister roared in response: 'We'll give 'em shells!' ... The food quickly became a bone of contention at the camp, as it was suspected that the cooks were selling the best meat to local tradesmen, leaving the recruits with the rough and fatty remains. A near riot ensued."* (From the Town Hall to the Boar's Head, by Sam Eedle, 2002) The Pioneer unit trained here for three months and the regiment served on the battlefields of France and Flanders from 1916 to 1918. As well as infantry work, they were paid an extra *"tuppence"* a day for digging trenches, laying barbed wire and building camps for other troops.

As well as the Gloucesters, three other Battalions from the Warwicks and the Worcesters, each of a thousand men, plus sections of the Royal Engineers, all camped on the commons and golf links along Peachfield Road, also training on the hills above. Malvern became a garrison town and armaments were manufactured at the Morgan Motor Works in Malvern Link, while drill halls were provided in Malvern College and St James' public school in West Malvern.

The battle casualties on the Western Front were enormous and seven hospitals were set up in the Malverns to treat some of the wounded.

The War Memorial in Malvern Priory

"Over 2,000 men were treated in Red Cross and naval hospitals, while 500 Belgians were accommodated after the invasion of their country." (A History of Malvern, Brian Smith, 1964) The police were frequently called to Cowleigh Road to break up fights between quarrelling Flemish and French speaking Belgians. There were calls for volunteers to replace the huge losses on the front and for women to fill the jobs they had vacated, as well as to nurse the injured. Many men and women of all classes from the Malverns volunteered, but four hundred and fifty of the local servicemen were killed in action. In total over nine and a half million military personnel and nearly seven million civilians died in the First World War, with about twenty one million people wounded. The famous poem by Lawrence Binyon *"For the Fallen - They shall not grow old, as we that are left grow old"*, which is heard on every Remembrance Day, was set to music by Elgar in *"The Spirit of England"* in 1916. To celebrate the end of the *"Great War"*, on 25th July 1919, many of Malvern's residents flocked to join in the torchlight procession to light a memorial bonfire on the Worcestershire Beacon.

Meanwhile, aristocratic anxiety had again increased when the Bolshevik revolution in Russia resulted in the abdication and shocking murder of King George's cousin, Tsar Nicolas II and his family in 1918. Since the time of Henry III, the Hornyold family had held large estates in Worcestershire, but now these were broken up to be sold off. In 1919 the heirs of the Duke of Gandolfi Hornyold divided the estate into five hundred lots for development. They sold most of Malvern Wells including Holy Well, much of North Malvern including the Tank and drinking spout, plus the farms and mansion house at Blackmore Park.

1887 Jubilee, Queen Victoria's extended family, Malvern Priory

After the war the boundaries of the Malverns were extended by new housing estates on the newly acquired land, with many residents buying cars to spend their leisure time touring the hills and local region. In 1894 in Malvern Link, the Santler brothers had made what is thought to be the first four-wheeled petrol-driven British motorcar. Production of Morgan

Charles Santler (left) in his old "Malvernia" car in a Malvern parade, c1920

cars had also begun here in 1909 and with a new spirit of enterprise, by 1919 they had not only launched their first four-seater family car but had also begun producing sports cars from their new Pickersleigh Road factory. A hundred years later these famous cars are still being custom built here, now under the direction of Charles Morgan.

Determined to enjoy themselves now that the war was over, many visitors travelled here by train on Great Western Railway day excursions, which extended from Cheltenham, Gloucester, Birmingham and Hereford to Malvern Link station. Three times a year on Bank Holidays, thousands flooded onto Cockshot Common below the Nags Head to enjoy all the fun of Mr Marshall's huge fair with its noisy beer tents, boxing booths, jugglers, fortune tellers, side shows and steam-driven carousel rides. Other attractions sometimes appeared, including a commemorative army Tank parked for a time on a plinth at Link Top. In 2006 Michael Gardener, then in his eighties, recalled as a child peering into the open jaws of an enormous dead whale, brought here on the back of a truck and covered inside and out with refrigeration pipes. One strange 'cabinet of curiosities' continued to arrive intermittently on Victoria Park until the 1950s. Shelved in a large tent were dozens of glass jars containing deformed animal foetuses preserved in formaldehyde, including two-headed kittens and Siamese-twin piglets. Otherwise healthy live sheep and pigs, with extra but useless legs, were penned nearby. Circuses of performing animals also came annually to the Link Common. To gain extra publicity the elephants were paraded down to drink the spring water from the horse trough that was then on the corner of Pickersleigh Road.

Many families also enjoyed hiring donkeys, often from Alice Betteridge in Happy Valley, to ride up to the Beacon summit and see the *"Toposcope"* designed by Elgar's friend Troyte Griffith, and then to take tea at the Beacon Café or at St Ann's Well. Every day *"Blind George"* Pullen played his harmonium here, or a Dulcitone with bell-like notes, often accompanied by the combined voices and dancing of happy visitors. In Great Malvern the more refined strains of live music could be heard all summer long from orchestras playing outdoors

Alice Betteridge at work courtesy Bannisters

in the Abbey and Rose Bank Gardens, or in Priory Park and on the Assembly Rooms' terrace. Visitors were attracted inside this elegant building with its huge windows, reminiscent of Crystal Palace, to attend events in the versatile Great Hall, which could function as a theatre, a concert hall or a ballroom. In 1936 Waldo and Muriel Lanchester founded another popular theatre on *"The Promenade"*, opposite Holly Mount Church, having also created the performers, their unique *"Lanchester Marionettes"* much loved by children and still sought after by many adult collectors.

144

'Victory', war memorial by Richard Goulden in front of Great Malvern Library

Chapter XIII

A Fountain, a Festival and the Famous

espite much opposition, another local Doctor, Henry Jacob, campaigned tirelessly for the public ownership of the town's entertainment centre, the Assembly Rooms and Winter Gardens, as part of his *"Brighter Malvern"* regeneration scheme. In 1927 he became Chairman of the Urban District Council and finally succeeded in purchasing the site for £17,000, bringing it into public ownership. But after a nervous breakdown during this stressful process, Dr Jacob died the following year. By 1930 the friends of this much loved local G.P., had

raised enough subscriptions from the public to install an expensive memorial fountain in the centre of the new Pump Room, on a pure white marble plinth, pedestal and basin with tall bronze urns at each corner. This fulfilled his wish that Malvern spring water, piped down from the hills, could be drunk by the general public when visiting the Theatre. This bronze sculpture of four water babies is by Richard Goulden, who also created the beautiful winged figure on the War Memorial at the Library. It was unveiled in June 1931 by Sir Stanley Baldwin, Earl of Bewdley and the Conservative Prime Minister and soon became the focal point for rendezvous and flirtations, as well as for taking the waters.

Goulden had trained at the Royal College of Art and at first was well known for his portraits, such as the figure of the painter George Frederick Watts in front of the Victoria & Albert Museum and the Margaret MacDonald memorial in the centre of Lincolns Inn Fields. This famous figure group is of a woman surrounded by nine cherubic children that are very similar to those in Malvern. It was built to commemorate Ramsay MacDonald's wife, a social reformer and suffragette who died in 1911, before he became the first Labour Prime Minister. But at the age of thirty seven Goulden went on active service to the front line in France, serving with the Royal Engineers from 1914 to 1919, where he was 'mentioned in dispatches'. After the war Goulden's work changed to focus on creating many significant war memorials, including those at Dover, Gateshead, Kingston on Thames, St John at Hackney, Reigate, St Michael's Redhill and inside the Garden Court of the Bank of England in London.

By 1929 in Malvern, the terrace and Theatre buildings were substantially

Festival Director Sir Barry Jackson

rebuilt and the Malvern Festival was then created. *"Sir Barry Jackson (who had a house on the Malvern Hills) was doubtless already planning his drama festival, which started in 1929. He probably agreed with the council some drastic alterations. The auditorium floor was raked, and a circle was added. The proscenium arch was widened and a "fly tower" erected. ... The first Malvern Drama festival lasted for a fortnight from August 19th 1929 and was dedicated to Bernard Shaw."* (A Brief History of the Malvern Festival Theatre, by Gerald Morice, 1979)

Sir Barry was the visionary founder of the Birmingham Repertory Theatre in 1913, providing a platform for new writers and modern productions, as well as experimenting with traditional theatre. Born in 1879, he had travelled in Europe during his teens, where he learnt French and began to paint. Although he wanted to become an artist, his wealthy industrialist father persuaded him to take a job in an architect's office in Birmingham, but he had already begun writing and performing plays with a group of friends as the amateur *"Pilgrim Players"*. By 1917 he had built a house called *"Blackhill"* at the Wyche, as he found the area both relaxing and inspiring. From 1929 to 1937 he collaborated

with Roy Limbert, the Malvern Theatre manager, to put on an annual summer festival of modern productions, showcasing the plays of George Bernard Shaw.

Shaw wrote several new plays especially for the festivals, and five of his plays, including *"The Apple Cart"* written at Blackhill, had their British premier at Malvern. An ardent socialist, Shaw had joined the Fabian Society in 1884 and wrote many pamphlets for them, including *"Socialism for Millionaires"* in 1900. He had become known as a political activist against World War 1, writing pieces such as *"The Rights of Man"*, and *"Common Sense About the War"*. A believer in gradual change through democratic socialism, not war or revolution, nearly all his work addressed prevailing social problems, including equal rights for men and women, class privilege, social hypocrisy and exploitation of

Wood engraving by Russian artist M. Pikov

the working classes. He often presented these issues with a strong vein of comedy and incisive wit, which made them entertaining and more palatable to those in the upper classes.

Shaw had been awarded the Nobel Prize for Literature in 1925 but wanted to refuse it, as he had no desire for public honours. The citation praised his work as *"marked by both idealism and humanity, its stimulating satire often being infused with a singular poetic beauty"*. He only accepted the prize after his wife argued that it was a tribute to Ireland, his birthplace, and he then donated the monetary award to fund the translation of August Strindberg's works from Swedish into English. Shaw admired the Union of Soviet Socialist Republics (USSR), travelling there in 1931 to meet Stalin. In contrast, in 1938 he received an Oscar for *"Pygmalion"* as the Film of the Year *"My Fair Lady"*, and in the same year the world premiere of his play *"Geneva"* was presented at Malvern.

Errol Flynn in the Festival Brochure

In 1934 one young aspiring actor appeared here in seven small 'walk-on' parts in five different festival plays, including *"Doctor Faustus"* by Marlowe. His name was Errol Flynn. His charm, good looks and enthusiasm were infectious and he proved very popular among the young women in the audience. Within a year he was signed up by Warner Brothers, appearing in two minor movie roles and then in the leading role of the early Hollywood 'talkie' *"Captain Blood"*, with a nineteen year old Olivia de Havilland. In New York in December 1935, with no expectations of great success, he and his wife Lili left the film's premier screening to go clubbing. Although Flynn had performed his role with more energy than dramatic skill, he became an overnight sensation as Captain Blood and the film was nominated for Best Picture.

Another festival performer was the little known Stewart Grainger from the Birmingham Repertory Theatre. Here he met Elspeth March, a leading actress with the company, who became his first wife. In Malvern John Rae recalled that *"Many cricket matches were organised between the locals and the visitors: in one match, organised by Walter Meade-King, Stewart Grainger batted and was bowled first ball by Walter, but it was Walter who was roundly booed by all the young ladies!"* (*Malvern Between the Wars by Frederick Covins, 1981*) After years of theatre work, in 1933 he made his film debut as an extra. At the beginning of the Second World War Grainger was invalided out of the army suffering from stomach ulcers. His first major film role was not until 1943, in the period melodrama *"The Man in Grey"*, which helped to make him a huge star.

As well as Shaw, many other writers visited Malvern in the 1930s and J. B. Priestly, then a critic and novelist, presided over the opening ceremony of the first summer festival. In 1933 he wrote the travelogue *"English Journey"*, an account of his observations when travelling through the country, but he then began writing satirical plays. He became well known as a dramatist with socialist views, writing a series of plays that enthralled West End theatre audiences. W. H. Auden also came to Malvern in this period, teaching at the Downs School in Colwall for three years. He was a much loved eccentric teacher, famously taking his bed out on to the lawn one summer to write. He wrote many poems here including *"The Malverns",* a long poem about the hills and their views. During his early career in England he was a strong advocate of socialism and Freudian psychoanalysis. Generally considered the greatest English poet of the twentieth century, his work has had a major influence on generations of poets in Britain and America.

Shaw Festival goers on the terrace of the theatre in the mid 1930's

The Shaw Festival became a popular part of the social calendar attracting rich, famous, fashionable and cultured visitors to the town, with its programme growing to include a month of plays, concerts, films, lectures, balls, dances, and dinners, plus private parties, parties, parties. Famous visitors ranged from J.B. Priestly, Yvonne Artaud, Dame Laura Knight and Sir Edward Elgar, to Arthur Askey, Alastair Sim, George Robey and Elsie and Doris Waters (Gert and Daisy). With late night trains laid on to London and Birmingham, the festival continued annually throughout the *"Great Depression"* of the thirties until the outbreak of the Second World War. But although the theatre company enjoyed touring here from Birmingham and found the plays worthwhile, the festivals were expensive to produce and in Sir Barry's opinion *"were not received gratefully by the people of Malvern"*. He resigned in 1937. Jackson and Shaw remained close friends and their numerous letters to each other are held in the Birmingham City Archives. As well as advice and ideas, Shaw often sent acorns, which Sir Barry planted, resulting in a group of oak trees growing at Blackhill. The Mulberry tree that Shaw planted in the Winter Gardens was destroyed in a storm in the 1990s, but its seedlings are being nurtured and may one day grow here again.

Sir Edward Elgar became a notable figure at the festival in the early

Elgar bronze in Malvern town centre. 2000

1930s. This great composer had lived in the Malverns for a total of twelve years; coming first to live in Malvern Link in June 1891, moving to Malvern Wells for five years from 1899 and keeping a second home in nearby Storridge until 1903. He was made Master of the King's Music in 1924 while living in the village of Kempsey, Worcestershire.

He was the first composer to make extensive audio recordings of his own compositions, under contract to HMV. In November 1931 Elgar was filmed by Pathé News conducting a recording session of his *"Pomp and Circumstance March"* No. 1 at the opening of the famous Abbey Road Studios in London. Years before he had conducted the first rendition of this piece to the children at the Wyche School. But after the words of *"Land of Hope and Glory"* were added, he had grown to dislike the popularity of this tune, which he felt had become a jingoistic song, not in keeping with the tragic loss of life in the war. When recording his

"Violin Concerto" in 1932, the aging composer worked with the American violinist Yehudi Menuhin, who was then only 16 years old. Many years later Menuhin still warmly remembered his association with the famous composer.

Sir Edward had found much of the inspiration for his music when walking or cycling around the Malvern Hills. *"My idea is that there is music in the air, music all around us, the world is full of it and you simply take as much as you require."* He dedicated one of his late works, *"Severn Suite"*, to his friend Bernard Shaw, who eventually persuaded the BBC to commission a third symphony from Elgar, although this piece

was never completed. Elgar died of cancer in Worcester in 1934 and is buried with his wife Alice in St Wulstan's Churchyard, Little Malvern. The tiny cottage where he was born in Lower Broadheath, Worcestershire, is now the Elgar Birthplace Museum, devoted to recording and celebrating his life and work.

152

Detail of an unfinished oil painting 'Sheep-shearing in the lee of the hills', c1930, inscribed Dame Laura Knight on the reverse side © *Rose Garrard*

Chapter XIV

Refuge in a Safe Haven

Sir Winston Churchill, First Lord at the Admiralty, had decided in 1938 that Malvern College was to be their headquarters in the event of war. Immediately after the Second World War against Germany was declared in September 1939, the College and its boy pupils were hurriedly moved out to Blenheim Palace, the home of the Duke of Marlborough. Following the fall of France in May 1940, many French refugees fled to Britain, including General De Gaulle himself, who set up his government-in-exile in London. Although most of the French troops were stationed near Bewdley, in autumn 1940 De Gaulle chose part of Malvern College as the headquarters for his 'École Militaire' to train Free French officer cadets, and he visited them here in 1942. The cadets consisted of a group of 211 young boys, aged 14 to 17, who took part in anti invasion manoeuvres with the local Home Guard. Forty eight of the officer graduates were subsequently killed in Europe before war ended.

Many of Malvern's other private schools were requisitioned to house hundreds of British evacuees trying to avoid the German bombing raids on the south coast and London. During the early part of the war, when

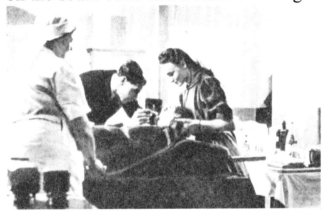

A Doctor and nurses examine a war casualtv

the invasion of Britain was expected hourly, the surviving Dutch forces also operated with the local Home Guard in the Malverns, as part of the anti-invasion force. From 1942 five American Army Hospitals were built on the fringes of the town, with railway sidings provided to deliver the many injured. Each hospital housed about two thousand U.S. soldiers, swelling the town's population to thirty thousand. After the Allies' invasion of Europe in 1944, hospital trains delivering injured patients became a familiar sight passing through Malvern's railway stations.

The first air raid on Coventry in 1940

Even after the liberation of Holland that year, Dutch soldiers continued to be sent here, occupying a former U.S. hospital at Wood Farm near Malvern. Although Malvern was on the flight corridor for German planes on route to Coventry and the industrialised Midlands, a total of no more than sixteen bombs were dropped onto the area. It's said these were merely jettisoned by the German bombers on their way back to Europe, most falling on the outskirts of Malvern Link and one damaging the Willow Spring when it fell beside Wyche Cutting.

In the 1930s Dame Laura Knight often spent time in the Malverns, staying at the Mount Pleasant, the British Camp Hotel, or at Sir Barry Jackson's home when she was visiting the Malvern Festival. At this time Laura Knight was the most prominent woman artist in Britain and

Laura Knight with Bernard Shaw at Lawnside School

the first woman to be elected to the Royal Academy since 1760. In 1929 she had been made a Dame Commander of the Order of the British Empire. As Sir Barry's houseguest she met authors, playwrights, actors, dancers, aristocrats and notables from all walks of life. Laura had started life in poverty, become artistically and financially successful, not only developing lasting friendships with the rich and famous, but also with the farm and factory workers, circus folk and gypsies, who were often the subject of her paintings. In 1934 the last Malvern donkey-woman, Mrs Alice Betteridge, spent four or five hours a day standing still with her donkey team, while they posed on the hills for Dame Laura, who recalled in her autobiography, *"carting materials up the wild of a Malvern hillside in late autumn when painting Mrs Betteridge's pony and donkeys."* (The Magic of a Line, by Dame Laura Knight, 1965)

In 1939 Dame Laura was approached by the War Artists' Advisory Committee regarding a painting commission on *"Britain's War Effort"* for a tiny fee, so she made several studies of members of the Women's Land Army at work in the fields around Malvern. She was then commissioned to produce a series of paintings, choosing to mostly record the changing roles of women during the war. Already in her sixties, for safety from the bombing raids, Dame Laura moved from London to stay at the Colwall Park Hotel in the Malverns from 1941 to 1945. She and her husband Harold also hired studios here

"Ruby Loftus screwing a Breech-ring", 1943
Permission of the Imperial War Museum, IWM ART LD 2850

for sixteen years after the war. She could easily travel from here to draw and paint her war-time subjects, workers in the industrialised Midlands and South Wales. J. B. Priestly's book *"British Women go to War"*, published in 1943, was illustrated by of many of these paintings.

Her success continued in 1946 with her harrowing commission to record the trials of the Nazi leaders at Nuremberg, when she was one of only three British women artists allowed to travel in Europe. After the war she was also elected to serve on the usually male preserve of the Royal Academy Hanging Committee, followed in 1952 by a commission for a painting of Princess Elizabeth. All this was achieved in an era when women were still fighting for equal rights and when many organizations and institutions excluded them. Her husband, the artist Harold Knight, died at the hotel in Colwall in 1961 and only after this did the

Dame Laura, Malvern, c1950

number of her works decline slightly. In the face of art criticism about

156

the range and variety of her works, towards the very end of her life she asked herself, *"Have I tried too many different media, too many different subjects? I do not know, except that my inner self continues to say, even today, go on, keep on trying something different."*

Three weeks after her death on 7th July 1970, aged 92, a memorial service was held for her at St James, a non-conformist church in Piccadilly,

Plaque at the Colwall Park Hotel

attended by many of her models as well as famous friends. Today Knight's works are keenly collected and recently *"Storm Over Our Town"*, an oil on canvas of Great Malvern from the Mount Pleasant Hotel, sold for £30,000 in Phillip Serrell's local auction rooms, selling in London for £49,950 a year later. On the 20th October 2009, Caroline McGhie reported in the Telegraph, *"Last month Dame Laura hit the headlines again when art expert Tom Rooth, prised away one of her canvases to reveal a painting hidden beneath which he described as "the find of a lifetime". It was a portrait of Sir Alfred Munnings by Laura's husband Harold, concealed possibly in order to avoid exacerbating Harold's jealousy of her intense friendship with Munnings."*

After the occupation of Ethiopia by Italy in 1936, Emperor Haile Selassie spent a small part of his exile in Malvern. He stayed briefly at the Abbey Hotel but spent most of his five years of exile in Bath. His attempts to gain support were largely unsuccessful until Italy entered the war on the German side in 1940. Early on in the war the Abbey Hotel was also adapted as the headquarters for the Ministry of Information, with the naval training and transmitting station of HMS Duke stationed nearby in St Andrew's Road. The Hotel also became the headquarters of the Belgian Army, when their country was overrun by the Germans and Malvern became a temporary home to the remnants of their forces. The Belgians were moved to South Wales when the Royal Telecommunications Research Division of the Royal Engineers arrived in the Hotel. During the invasion of Dunkirk and subsequent rescue of troops from the beaches, the army chiefs also came to the Abbey Hotel, while Malvern's many large houses accommodated some of the exhausted survivors.

In February 1942 British paratroops raided the German radar station at Bruneval, bringing back photographs and key pieces of radar equipment to analyse in the laboratory at the Telecommunications and Radar Establishment in Purbeck, Swanage. *"The scientists were very impressed and rather shocked by the quality of German engineering. The examination enabled them to work out how to jam the German radar and to fool it with false echoes to show 'ghost' forces. These electronic counter measures were key to the success of the D-Day*

Wurtzburg radar dish sited in Malvern Link © *Crown/Putley*

landings. ... Churchill thought that the Germans were going to raid the radar work in Purbeck, and ordered the establishment to leave the area before the next full moon." (Secret War in Purbeck, by Jonathan Penley and Dr B. Penley, Purbeck Radar Trust 2008)

The Malvern school boys returned briefly to the College, but in 1942 had to move out again when the T.R.E. from Purbeck moved into the College buildings to continue developing these top secret methods of detecting enemy aircraft. Then the R.R.D.E., the Radar Research and

T.R.E. huts built at Malvern College. 1942

Development Establishment, also moved here from Christchurch in Hampshire, into the R.A.F. base at Pale Manor Farm, North Site.

Temporary buildings for radar scientists in the grounds of Malvern College, with aerial masts for field trials in the distance, 1942 © *Purbeck Museum Radar Trust*

At Purbeck they had developed some crucial radar applications, including *"Ground Controlled Interception"* using radar tracking on *"Plan Position Indicators"* and cockpit radar systems which enabled British fighter planes to intercept the attacking German bombers in poor visibility or at night. At Malvern they now worked rapidly on developing anti-aircraft defences and new aerial offensive weapons, with a radar school for training R.A.F. officers based in College Road.

Female operator plotting both attacking bombers and defending fighter aircraft on the new radar 'Plan Position Indicator', © *Purbeck Museum Radar Trust*

The work included the development of micro-wave radar, which hugely increased the range and accuracy of detection. The T.R.E. director, A.P. or 'Jimmy' Rowe, invited senior individuals from the Air Ministry and Royal Air Force to 'think-tank' meetings called *"Sunday Soviets"*, to freely discuss ideas about these applications with the scientists and any potential problems, developing mutual trust and co-operation. Scientists from America then moved into the County Hotel, now Parkview, to work secretly on parallel offensive and defensive developments.

'Sunday Soviet' meeting at Malvern College, with Jimmy Rowe seated behind the desk, wearing glasses, *courtesy Jonathan Penley, © Purbeck Museum Radar Trust*

T.R.E. had also been working closely with MI6 in countering the Luftwaffe's navigational beam technology, in what became known as *"the battle of the beams"*, to hamper the enemy's ability to make the night bombing raids that were ravaging many British cities. *"As the war turned in Britain's favour, T.R.E. shifted its emphasis to guiding R.A.F. bombers to targets over Germany. It produced a grid of radar signals across Europe, which allowed bombers to navigate towards their targets. And its 'Oboe' system allowed controllers on the*

Fighting fires after German bomb damage at the corner of Birmingham New Street

ground to track and guide bombers with unprecedented accuracy – allowing the devastation of the Ruhr industries. On the night before D-Day it enabled bombers to silence the defensive coastal batteries. No less important was T.R.E.'s development of a radar system for spotting surfacing U-boats; this rendered them much more vulnerable to detection, and Hitler blamed it for German reverses in the battle of the Atlantic." (The Times, May 31, 2007)

As over 2,500 top scientists and staff had now been compulsorily billeted here, a Government Restriction Order made the Malverns a high security, restricted area, but otherwise it remained unscathed. Nothing about the presence or purpose of these non-combatants could be disclosed, and Malvern residents often resented these mysterious men being billeted into their homes. Many locals became very nervous about the nature of the scientists' work here, particularly after the first atomic bomb was dropped on Hiroshima in Japan on 6th August 1945, killing 74,000 people, but ending the war eight days later.

For many able-bodied servicemen returning to their bombed homes in British cities, house building and repairs became their new priority. But in the undamaged Malverns, new housing estates were built for the scientists, causing further local resentment. Some residents focused their concerns on the continuing secrecy of the Royal Radar Establishment, with rumours spreading of atomic experiments under the hills. This led to an open-day at the main site in the late 1950s, to try to allay people's fears about the scientists' work. Visitors were shown equipment inside some of the buildings, including a large room filled with rows of identical tall machines, whirring as they were fed with information from cards punched with holes. This was 'TREAC', one of the very first computers, a completely new technology to most residents. Like all the site workers, visitors were also issued with small plastic badges of various colours. On leaving, each badge was examined and only then was each visitor shocked to learn that its colour would have changed if we had been exposed to atomic radiation or x-rays. Not until the 1990s did it become publicly known that during the war some atomic research had taken place on the Malvern College grounds, at the Atomic Energy Research Establishment, based in a fenced enclosure of huts on today's green at the Lees. R.R.E. continued their work on telecommunications and radar research long after the war, with pioneer developments in the newer fields of the silicon chip, infra-red research, micro-waves, lasers, satellite communications and liquid crystal displays. Most of the establishment was privatised in 2001, becoming QinetiQ, an international defence technology company. It is still the largest single employer in the Malverns.

After the war, quarrying on the hills also became a major concern to many residents, threatening the ridge of the hills in several places, with violent twice-daily explosions regularly throwing rocks onto the streets and houses below Tank Quarry in North Malvern. This very hard Malvern stone, quarried from the hills by the Pyx Granite Company since the 1860s, was easily fragmented into the misshapen but usable blocks

Tank Quarry and Clock Tower c1920, courtesy B. Iles

that had been used for building many local Victorian houses. When crushed it was an ideal material for road building, both before and after the war. As a result of the continuing efforts of residents and the Malvern Hills Conservators since their founding in 1884, all quarrying was finally stopped in 1966. The Malvern Hills Act in 1924 had given the Conservators powers to prevent quarrying through the compulsory purchase of land and to make byelaws to restrict and regulate the existing quarrying operations, but until now its provisions had proved largely ineffective.

The quarrying left many ugly scars that changed the face of the hills forever, but the work force of the Conservators soon scrambled up the

Dangerously deep and cold waters in Gullet Quarry

rocks to plant native trees and shrubs, creating habitats for small wild animals and nesting sites for falcons and many other birds. Some of the dramatic quarries are now used for official courses in safe abseiling and rock climbing, but over the years these treacherous sites have also attracted other visitors who have ignored the dangers. Many injured people have had to be rescued, but some have been killed when climbing the loose rock faces, or drowned while swimming in the freezing waters of Gullet Quarry. But despite these dangers, for most people the Malverns continue to be a safe and beautiful haven.

162

'Ridgeway', oil on canvas by David Prentice, 2000

Chapter XV

Imagination in Millennium Malvern

alvern seems to have always attracted very imaginative people. The novelist C. S. Lewis was a pupil at Malvern College from 1913 and later used to walk on the Malvern Hills with his friend J. R. R. Tolkien. After drinking in a Malvern pub one winter evening, they were walking home along the woody hillside when a solitary gas lamp, shining out through the falling snow, caught their attention. Lewis used this magical image in his book *"The Lion, the Witch and the Wardrobe"* as his characters entered the realm of Narnia. His death, on 22nd November 1963, was overshadowed by the assassination of President John F. Kennedy on the same day, but the continuing debate over which was Lewis's actual gas lamp has helped to preserve them to the present day.

By the sixties and seventies many of the R.R.E. scientists had become permanent residents in the Malverns and often played a creative role in the continuing artistic initiatives in the local region. In 1989, while still working as a Scientific Officer at the newly named Defence Evaluation

European Union Chamber Orchestra at Malvern

and Research Agency, Peter Smith, a professionally trained singer and violinist, and a native of Malvern created the *"Autumn in Malvern Festival"*, Malvern's independent celebration of classical music and the arts. For twenty years Peter has presented exceptional British and European orchestras, musicians, writers, film-makers and visual artists in this major event throughout October every year. He also founded the *"Aldwyn Voices"* in Malvern in 1968 and under his artistic directorship they are now widely known for their broadcasts on BBC TV, Radio 3 and 4, and on the World Service.

This distinguished chamber choir was awarded the prestigious *"Kodaly Trophy"* for outstanding services to European choral music, presented by the BBC, Hungarian and EBU radio networks.

The professional visual artists, David and Dinah Prentice, moved to Malvern Wells in 1990 from Birmingham, where they had been instrumental in founding the first Ikon Gallery in 1965, with four others, *"to invigorate the city with progressive ideas about art"*. Once in Malvern they soon settled into their disciplined routine of daily work in their separate studios. At first both had been abstract painters, but 45

years on David has become an internationally renowned oil and water-colourist, widely known for his dramatic landscapes, often of the Malvern Hills ridge. A prolific painter, David has held over forty solo exhibitions of his work in commercial galleries throughout Britain since 1961. *"Over the past two decades, Solihull-born David has built up a considerable reputation among critics and collectors alike for his richly coloured, atmospheric paintings often described as being in the tradition of Constable and Turner. He has collected a raft of accolades, including prizes in the prestigious Singer & Friedlander – Sunday Times Watercolour Competition, no fewer than four times, most recently last year."* (Birmingham Post, by Ros Dodd, 2008)

David and Dinah working in their studios

Dinah Prentice, also a long respected artist, is now increasingly well known for her sewn works, which she began to develop in the 1970s, combining painting techniques with textile constructions of silk to make

Dinah Prentice at work on 'Billowing Maenads' in 2008

huge wall-hangings. These usually explore personal and political issues and events through her basis in feminist theory. One of her largest works, *"Laced Threads"*, is permanently installed in the Rotunda Gallery in the Aston Webb Building at Birmingham University.

Dinah regularly shows in public spaces worldwide, and in 2008 created an installation of a 100 foot long paper scroll of images and text in the Buttermarket opposite the Ikon, organised by Number Nine Gallery. *"It's called 'Fragments' because it reviews the nature of cutting, editing and reassembly in my work and shows some of the core themes that have influenced me,"* she said. *"The manipulation of a woven limp surface which needs support, be it a wall or ceiling or armature, is incredibly human – a sort of witness to vulnerability – hence the use of silk chiffon gauze to give a 'thin, fine and airy' feel."* Having travelled from London to view Dinah's installation, a representative of the Victoria & Albert is now planning an exhibition of her work in the Museum in the near future.

Dennis Neale with 'Snowcake' the puppet
Courtesy Malvern Gazette, a Newsquest publication

In November 1999 *"The Theatre of Small Convenience"* opened in a former Victorian public lavatory in Edith Walk, at the centre of Great Malvern. Here its founder, Dennis Neale, a talented puppeteer and playwright, presents dramatic performances by both amateur and professional actors, of puppetry, poetry, story-telling, music and opera, often as part of his unique short plays for children of all ages. The wonderfully ingenious puppets and sets are made by Dennis from recycled found-materials. With his partner Ros as usher, the theatre has a capacity of 12 people seated or 16 standing. It entered the Guinness Book of World Records in 2002 as the smallest built theatre in the world.

Malvern is also the home of the *"Malvern Fringe Festival"*, one of the

oldest fringe festivals in the world, originally founded in 1977 as a popular alternative musical event, on the fringe of the Elgar Festival. It aims to bridge the generation gap with an annual town procession on May Day and three days of live local bands, plus other musical events throughout the year.

In 1995 the *"Malvern Festival Theatre"* came under the directorship of Nic Lloyd and two years later was again closed for major refurbishment, following a 5.2 million pound award from the National Lottery Fund. The 1920s balustrades, covered terraces and Pump Room were swept away, transforming the building and improving the Theatre acoustics. But in the face of considerable public opposition, the open-plan interior was controversially named *"The New Space"* and then renamed *"The Forum"*. On April 24th 1998, the first performance in the Forum Theatre was Beethoven's violin concerto played by the famous virtuoso Nigel Kennedy, then living in West Malvern with his first wife and son.

A boy prodigy, Kennedy was a pupil of Yehudi Menuhin, who lived from 1916 to 1999 and had been a friend and admirer of Sir Edward Elgar. *"What is less well-known is that Kennedy also caught the attention of the great jazz violinist Stephane Grappelli, who he looked upon as his jazz godfather. Although temperamentally and professionally polar opposites, Menuhin and Grappelli were close friends and recording partners, which left Kennedy ideally placed to absorb the influence of both. "Yehudi and Stephane were at the height of their powers when I got to hang out with them as a kid," he says. "One day I'd see Grappelli getting ready for a gig with his brandy and a spliff; on another it would be Menuhin with his muesli and his wife combing his hair."* (Kennedy interviewed for the Guardian by Alfred Hicklin, September 2006)

Nigel Kennedy and Caleb jamming in Malvern © *Jem Vipond 2000*

Regulars in West Malvern's pubs and the *"Working-men's Club"* had become familiar with often brilliant impromptu sessions, where Kennedy improvised with local musicians, sometimes raising money for local causes. To celebrate the end of the century, Kennedy invited many of his creative Malvern friends to the Grove in Avenue Road for an enormous millennium party, filled with extraordinary live music. Close to twelve o'clock a small group of visual artists then met up on Foley Terrace, watching as, at the stroke of midnight, a magical sea of fireworks sparkled for miles across the Severn Vale below.

The Jacob Fountain had remained in place in the Malvern Theatres from 1930 until the redevelopment, but in 1997 this valuable bronze sculpture was discovered discarded on the building site and it was rescued as a result of the efforts of Rose Garrard, sculptor, and Carly Tinkler, then the

168

Council Planning Officer. The builders reported they had been offered £500 for it! The square marble base had already been broken up and the pipe work destroyed, although the leaking spring water is said to have soon filled the newly dug lift-shaft and had to be continuously pumped into Swan Pool. The much-damaged fountain can now be found tucked out of the way, surrounded by stored chairs and litter bins in a corner of the restaurant, sadly without any supply of Malvern spring water.

In August 1996, as part of their Regeneration Strategy, the Malvern Hills District Council led by Councillor John Ford, had appointed a Spa Water Strategy Working Group, chaired by Councillor John Tretheway, to address the role that water could play in the revitalisation of the town centre. Jim Black from Severn Trent Water, Cora Weaver and Bruce Osborne, local historians, were among those who joined the Working Group with Carly Tinkler, a landscape architect, volunteering their expertise on Malvern's ancient springs and water systems. In response to newspaper appeals for ideas, by June 1996 internationally known sculptor Rose Garrard, then living in London, had independently proposed to the MHDC the creation of a new sculpture trail by nationally known sculptors, on lost spring sites throughout the town centre. At the first meeting of the Spa Working Group on 20th September 1996, Rose was invited to present ideas for her *"Malvern Water Trail"*. The Group then identified two main objectives; the restoration and conservation of the existing springs of the Malverns, and the establishment of sites for new

'Malvhina' drinking spout unveiled by MHDC Chair, Pat Raven, September 1998

town centre water features. The District Council decided that it did not have sufficient resources to pursue both routes and, as their main objective was to regenerate Great Malvern town centre, only proceeded with the creation of new water features.

In October 1997 the District Council commissioned Rose to undertake research in a two month long Artist's Residency here, consulting the public who mapped 245 remembered water sites around the hills as part of this *"Spring Water Arts Project"*. During her residency Rose was also asked to create a new spring water drinking spout, *"Malvhina"*, unveiled on 4th September 1998, followed in 1999 by a commission for the *"Enigma Fountain"*, both on Belle Vue Island. Due to changes following local elections and despite available Arts Council grants, the new Council failed to commission further sculptors.

The Enigma Fountain unveiled by Prince Andrew on 26ᵗʰ May 2000

This municipal fountain in the town centre was designed to celebrate Sir Edward Elgar, his music the *"Enigma Variations"* written in Malvern in 1898, and Malvern's pure spring water. To celebrate the Millennium, despite continuous rain, the town was filled with people and flags to greet Prince Andrew when he arrived to unveil the *"Enigma Fountain"*, which is fed by natural water pressure from three springs on the hills high above the town. Elgar's composition is made up of fourteen sections, each a musical portrait of one of his friends, represented as an 'enigma' by their initials on the score. These letters are each carved on the fourteen sides of the fountain in a facsimile of Elgar's own handwriting. They begin and end with the initials of Elgar himself and his wife Alice, meeting at the feet of his bronze figure. Carved above these is a line from a poem by Arthur O'Shaughnessy, *"We are the music makers, we are the dreamers of dreams, ... "*, which Elgar set to music as *"The Music Makers"* in 1912.

In order to take forward the other main objective of the Spa Working Group, the restoration of Malvern's historic springs and wells, a large group of interested local people gathered together in September 1998 and the Malvern Spa Association (MSA) was formed. John Ford was elected as the dynamic first MSA Chairman from 1998 to 2002, sadly dying of cancer in 2006. In 2002 all the MSA's detailed research on the history and current condition of twenty springs was given to the Malvern Hills Area of Outstanding Natural Beauty office and four years later the AONB received a grant of over £270,000 from the Heritage Lottery Fund. But as many of the springs are on the hills, the project application was coupled with a separate larger grant for cattle grazing on the hills, awarded to the Malvern Hills Conservators under the directorship of Ian Rowat, chaired by John Tretheway and then Ray Roberts.

The Clock Tower after restoration.

In the face of global warming, by 2010 the MSA had continued for twelve years to help in the restoration of twenty spring water sites as part of the combined *"Malvern Heritage Project"*. Carly Tinkler was the second MSA Chair until 2006, when Rose Garrard became the Chairperson. With David Armitage of the AONB, who managed the springs' restoration project and budget, the MSA's volunteers worked tirelessly to try to ensure that the springs were restored to the highest possible standards. Pure spring water has now been re-established at the Clock Tower, the Lower Wyche Spout, the Jubilee Fountain, the Royal Well and West Malvern Tap, and with Malvhina this has doubled the number of functioning drinking water spouts around the Malverns. The project was completed under the present MSA Chairman Dr John Harcup, a historian and former local GP.

Repairs to the neglected structures and sites were also made at St Ann's Well pool and side spout, Hayslad, Lord Sandy's Spout in Malvern Link, Earl Beauchamp's Spout, North Malvern spout beside the Clock Tower, Barnards Green Trough, Weaver's Well, Ellerslie Fountain, Lower Wyche Trough, Wynds Point and Wyche Spouts, Willow Spring, St James' Church Spout, and Westminster Bank Springs. In December 2009, the last of the Lottery funding had also enabled the AONB and MSA to restore the public spout, the 'sanctuary' and well rooms at Holy Well.

From the Original Holy Well

WHEN YOU DRINK Cuff's "Still Malvern" Water, you drink "The Water of Health" from one of the highest Springs in England — pure because uncontaminated by lower surface impurities — and the Spring-Well that first established the fame of Malvern as a Health Resort.

Ask Everywhere for

Cuff's 'Still Malvern'

unrivalled as a Health and Table Water. Medically prescribed for Rheumatism, Kidney, Bladder, Bowel and Nerve Troubles. Price 8/6 per doz., from Wine Merchants, Chemists, Grocers, or direct from

J. H. CUFF & CO., MALVERN WELLS

Write for interesting Free Booklet.

They also added a new spring water heritage information display and helped to re-establish a commercial bottling plant at the site.

Mike and Marian Humm had bought the well house and adjacent cottage in 1999, following the death of previous owner John Parkes who had

restored the well in the 1970s with his wife Thelma. *"The best part of a decade on Mike has now achieved his dream, with the Holy Well currently producing about 600 bottles of water, both still and sparkling, every day. Rhys, who joined his father as a director of the business in February, said: "The demand is pretty good at the moment. The history and providence of the product is a huge help, as is the fact that this is the original source of Malvern water." (Malvern Gazette, by Tarik Al Rasheed, November 2009)*

Since the mid 1990's the respected artist Olwen Tarrant has also lived in the Malverns, working in her studio in Upper Welland below the Malvern Hills. *"I love Elgar's music and it is wonderful to listen to it at home looking at the scene which inspired him; I think, in a very modest way, that it inspires me, too."* She won her first award while still a student at the Sir John Cass Art College in East London, with a painting of a morning commuter train to Liverpool Street station. The judge was Sir Charles Wheeler, former President of the Royal Academy, who prophesied a successful career for her and bought the painting for his own

collection. It was the first of many prizes that she has gained for both her painting and sculpture, including the Alan Gourley, Cornelissen, and Llewellyn Alexander awards.

Having shown regularly in the annual exhibition of the Royal Institute of Oil Painters in London, Olwen became the only woman in its 125-year history to ever be elected its President, serving from 1999 to 2004. For many years women were even excluded from membership of the institute, and one of the first women to break through this discrimination was Dame Laura Knight in the 1930's. Other famous artists who have shown with the society include Walter Sickert, Auguste Rodin and Henri Fantin-Latour. In 2007 Olwen won another prestigious award for one of her oil paintings, a portrait of a woman in a studio, entitled *"I am what I am"*. It was chosen as *"the judge's favourite"* for the A & K Wilson Award in an exhibition in the Mall Galleries in London. She was presented with the award by actress Maureen Lipman and commented *"It's always nice to have your work recognised. I was surprised because I didn't even know I was on the shortlist."* She has lectured on painting and sculpture throughout her career and exhibited her work in galleries across the country, showing her work for the first time in Great Malvern in 2010, at the Library.

A wide variety of resident musicians also add to Malvern's rich heritage. David Lowe is a contemporary musician and professional composer living in West Malvern, who focuses primarily on music for television and radio. One of the most renowned composers based in the UK, he is a member of the British Academy of Film and Television Arts (BAFTA) and the British Academy of Composers and Songwriters. In 1997, David released his debut album, *"Dreamcatcher"*, described as *"Global music"* with *"beautiful ethnic sounds and voices, mixed with cool western beats and textures"*. He performed a live mix that year at the first Thames River Festival in London, which accompanied a record breaking tightrope walk across the river. His album *"Straight...to Number One"* was chosen by Apple to launch the 'iTunes' site in the USA, where every track has now been used in films, television or commercials. Among his many projects, Lowe also co-produced an album for poet Roger McGough setting some of the poetry to music. In 2005 he was awarded an honorary doctorate by Staffordshire University and the following year was commissioned to write the

music for the BAFTA Film and Television Awards and for the BBC's coverage of the Winter Olympics. His work includes all the current themes for the BBC News, their regional, national and international broadcasts on both TV and Radio, plus the present theme for the BBC World Service. His numerous compositions for TV programmes include musical identities for *"The One Show"*, *"Panorama"*, *"Wildlife on One"*, *"Countryfile"* and the motoring programme *"Fifth Gear"*.

Paul Farrer is another talented British composer living in West Malvern. Born in Worcester, Paul began working in a professional recording studio after leaving school at sixteen, while continuing to play piano, clarinet, violin, saxophone and trumpet. He began by creating jingles for radio stations before writing music for many television programmes and movies, including scores for the Disney movie *"Toy Story"*, ITV's *"Dancing On Ice"* and Jonathan Dimbleby's *"A Kosovo Journey"*. He has been awarded the BMI's Composer Award, previously given to artists such as John Lennon and Eminem. After being approached by the BBC

in 2000, he also wrote the music for *"The Weakest Link"*, presented by Anne Robinson. This has become one of BBC TV's most successful shows, currently playing in over ninety-six countries. As Paul receives royalties every time the programme is broadcast he has become a rich man. He soon moved from his small semi-detached cottage to a mansion in the Malverns, with his wife and two young children. Paul said *"Thanks to the show, I could have retired some years ago. My family are as baffled as I am about the success of it all. I'm really not a flash person."* He conceives much of his music, including the *"Walk of Shame"* theme heard throughout the show, while he is out walking on the Malvern Hills.

Having also purchased Raglan House in West Malvern, by 2007 Paul had replaced it with a purpose-built professional recording studio, *"The Music Mint"*, and a children's nursery for the community. It was when laying the foundations of this very modern facility that the builders uncovered many ancient fossils of small marine creatures on a shingle beach, dating from the time of the Silurian Sea, six hundred million years ago.

Fossils from the Silurian Sea, found in West Malvern in 2005, *Courtesy Paul Farrer*

As well as continuing to attract talented residents, the Malverns have given birth to many other successful new projects and events, too numerous to include here, often relying on generous help from multitudes of enthusiastic local volunteers. Through many of these initiatives and people, the history of Malvern continues to develop in imaginative ways, often inspired by the natural as well as man-made assets from its unique past. Long may they all continue in the making of Malvern's future.

BIBLIOGRAPHY

1660 to 1697 - Worcestershire Sessions Rolls

1674 - History and Antiquities of the University of Oxford, by Anthony Wood

1781 - History of Worcestershire, by Dr T. Nash, London, John White

1817 - General History of Malvern, John Chambers, Longman, Hurst, Rees & Orme

1824 - A Description of Malvern, by Mary Southall, Longman, Hurst and Co.

1829 - A Concise History of the City and Cathedral of Worcester, by T. Eaton

1831 - Topographical Dictionary of England, by Samuel Lewis

1852 - Antiquities & Folklore of Worcestershire, by Jabez Allies

1856 - Notes and Queries for Worcestershire, by John Noake, Longman & Co.

1866 - The Monastery & Cathedral of Worcester, by John Noake, Longman & Co.

1868 - Guide to Worcestershire, by John Noake, Longman & Co.

1875 - The British Camp, by James Mc Kay, Kessinger

1877 - Worcestershire Relics, by John Noake, Longman & Co.

1882 - Notes from The Feoffee Book at Tewksbury, by Mr H.P. Moore

1883 - Hanley Castle by W.S. Symonds, Rector of Pendock

1885 - Some of the Antiquities of 'Moche' Malvern, by James Nott

1886 - Guide to Malvern, by Norman May, Norman May & Co. Ltd

1889 - The Shadow of the Ragged-Stone, by Charles F. Grindrod

1894 - Lansdown Manuscript, from Historic Worcestershire, by W. Salt Brassington

1895 - Malvern Priory Church, by James Nott, Thompson & Royal Library, Malvern

1897 - Notes from Worcestershire Medieval Tax Rolls, by Rev. F.J. Eld,

1901 - The Malvern Country, by Bertram Windle, Methuen & Co.

1904 - Malvern In and Near, by M. T. Stevens & Co

1906 - Ward Lock's Malvern Guide, Ward, Lock & Co. Ltd.

1913 - The Ancient Malvern Priory, by M. C. Stevens Ltd

1914 - Great Malvern Priory Church, by Rev. Anthony C. Deane, Bell & Sons

1924 - Malvern Priory Registers, Lecture by F.C.Morgan

1932 - A Worcestershire Book, by the Federation of Women's Institutes

1942 - Complete Works of Tacitus, 2nd century AD, Random House

1943 - Worcestershire in English History, by Alec Macdonald, Press Alliances Ltd.

1947 - History of the Worcester Royal Infirmary, by William H. McMenemey, Press Alliances Ltd

1948 - A Little City set on a Hill, by C.F. Severn Burrow, Priory Press, Malvern

1949 - Worcestershire, by L.T.C. Rolt, Robert Hale Ltd

1964 - A History of Malvern, by Brian S. Smith, Leicester University Press

1967 - Regional Archaeologies: The Severn Basin, by K.S. Painter, Heinemann

1968 - Malvern Country, by Vincent Waite, J.M. Dent & Sons

1970 - Customs and Folklore of Worcestershire, by Lavender M. Jones, Estragon

1979 - Worcestershire Archaeology & Local History Newsletter

1979 - A Brief History of the Malvern Festival Theatre, by Gerald Morice, (pamphlet)

1981 - Malvern Between The Wars, by Frederick Covins, Book Production Services

1991- Worcestershire's Hidden Past, Bill Gwilliam, Halfshire Books

1992 - The Folklore of Hereford & Worcester, by Roy Palmer, Logaston Press

1993 - Not the Least, the Story of Little Malvern, by Ronald Bryer, Hanley Swan

1994 - West Malvern, by Valerie Goodbury, self published

2000 - The Celts, by John Davies, Cassell and Co.

2002 - From the Town Hall to the Boar's Head, by Sam Eedle, published in the Tewkesbury Historical Society Bulletin No. 11

2004 - Report by the Archaeology Service of Worcestershire County Council,
2004 - The Black Death, by Francis Aidan Gasquet, Kessinger Publishing
2006 - Malvern Freemasonry and the Masonic Hall, R. Hall-Jones, First Paige Printers
2008 - Severn Bankside Survey, Worcestershire Archaeological Service
2008 - Secret War in Purbeck, by Jonathan Penley and Dr B. Penley, self-published
2009 - 20th Century Defences in Britain: The West Midland Region, by Colin Jones,
        Bernard Lowry and Mick Wilks, Logaston Press
2009 - Science comes to Malvern, by Ernest Putley, self published, Aspect Design

FURTHER INFORMATION

1992 - The Malvern Water Cure, by John Winsor Harcup, Winsor Fox Photos
1994 - Archiving My Own History, by Rose Garrard, Cornerhouse Gallery,
        Manchester
1994 - Aquae Malvernensis, by Cora Weaver & Bruce Osborne, self published
2005 - Images of England ; The Malverns, by Brian Iles, Tempus
2006 - Malvern Hill of Fountains, by Rose Garrard, Aspect Design
2007 - The Forest and Chase of Malvern, Pamela Hurle, Phillimore & Co.
2008 - Donkeys' Years on the Malvern Hills, by Rose Garrard, Aspect Design

FURTHER ILLUSTRATION CREDITS

Page 22   Portable Antiquities Scheme – www.finds.org. uk
Page 23   Kingdom of the Hwicce by TharkunColl, Wikipedia
Page 158 Emperor Haile Selassie from G. Eric and Edith Mason
             Photograph Collection, Library of Congress, USA

Green Man, Malvern Priory